1/10/99
CITY PRESS
7.95

D0128213

HOUSES BENEATH THE ROCK

1/10/99
CITY PRESS
7.95

HOUSES BENEATH THE ROCK

The Anasazi of Canyon de Chelly
and Navajo National Monument

Edited by
David Grant Noble

Ancient City Press
Santa Fe, New Mexico

© Copyright 1986 by School of American Research, P.O. Box 2188, Santa Fe, New Mexico 87504. Originally published as *Tsé Yaa Kin: Houses Beneath the Rock* by School of American Research.

For information address: Ancient City Press, P.O. Box 5401 Santa Fe, New Mexico 87502. Telephone (505) 982-8195.

Cover photo: White House Ruin, Canyon de Chelly 1991 by David Grant Noble.

Back Cover: Rock art figures, Canyon del Muerto. From photo by David Noble.

Assistant editor: Melinda Elliot

Cover design: Mary Powell

First Ancient City Press edition

Library of Congress Cataloging-in-Publication Data

Houses beneath the rock : the Anasazi of Canyon de Chelly and Navajo
    National Monument / edited by David Noble.—1st Ancient City Press ed.
      p.   cm.
    Originally published: Santa Fe, N.M. : School of American
    Research. 1986, in series: Exploration series.
      ISBN: 0-941270-72-6 :
      1. Pueblo Indians — Antiquities. 2. Navajo Indians — History.
    3. Cliff-dwellings — Arizona. 4. Chelly, Canyon de (Ariz.) — History.
    5. Canyon de Chelly National Monument (Ariz.) 6. Navajo National
    Monument (Ariz.) 7. Arizona — Antiquities. I. Noble, David Grant.
    E99.P9H74 1992   91-78069
    979.1'37 — dc20   CIP

10   9   8   7   6   5   4   3   2   1

Contents

TSÉ YAA KIN: Houses Beneath the Rock

by Jeffrey S. Dean

Kiet Siel cliff dwelling. Photo by William C. Stoughton, 1976. Courtesy National Park Service.

REMOTE AND ENIGMATIC, cliff dwellings epitomize the romance of southwestern archaeology. Concealed in the shadowed recesses of lonely canyons or nestled at the bases of high, wind-swept mesas, cliff dwellings exude an aura of exotic mystery. Protected by overhanging rock from the ravages of the elements, ancient hamlets and villages are preserved like insects in amber. Few people can resist the attraction of the brooding isolation and tantalizing condition of these settlements in the rock. Thus, the discovery in the late nineteenth century of spectacular cliff pueblos excited the imagination of the American public and resulted in the creation at Mesa Verde of the first national park devoted primarily to an archaeological theme. Prehistorians proved equally susceptible to the lure of cliff dwellings. Early archaeological exploration of the farther reaches of the northern Southwest was impelled largely by the quest for undiscovered cliff dwellings and fueled by the hope that their inaccessibility augured a high yield of artifacts for analysis and display.

Fascination with cliff dwellings arises from several sources. Many of these sites are situated in spectacular natural settings, whose scenic grandeur is widely appreciated. Mesa Verde National Park and Canyon de Chelly and Navajo national monuments are treasured as much for their natural beauty as for the cliff dwellings that are the ostensible reasons for their existence.

Laymen are drawn to cliff dwellings because, unlike amorphous mounds of rubble and broken pottery, these structures are easily recognizable for what they are—the abandoned homes of fellow human beings. The intact features of the cliff dwellings poignantly project the fundamental human experience across time, space, and cultural boundaries.

Although they share the reactions of laymen, archaeologists have a more arcane appreciation of cliff dwellings: they are prime sources of information. Because once human occupation ends, rock shelters undergo natural alterations different from those that occur at open sites, the former provide materials and data that both supplement and complement the information derived from the latter. For example, architectural features and relationships remain much more complete in cliff dwellings, and the excellent preservation provides a range of perishable items impossible to obtain from open sites. Well-preserved examples of basketry, cordage, textiles, hides, wooden and bone implements, maize, squash, beans, gourds, cotton, and wild plant and animal foods recovered from cliff dwellings have immeasurably enhanced knowledge of prehistoric southwestern technology, economics, and sociocultural organization. Small wonder, then, that generations of archaeologists have scoured remote canyons and isolated mesas for potentially rich sheltered sites.

Life in the Rock

Caves and overhanging cliffs have sheltered humans for as long as they have walked the earth. Around a million years ago in Asia, *Homo erectus* huddled around campfires in the caves of Chou Kou Tien. Much later, Neanderthal people in the Near East and western Europe utilized rock shelters for protection against the elements and beasts of prey. Subsequently, anatomically modern humans survived the long winters on the gelid fringes of the Ice Age glaciers by taking refuge in the caves of western Europe. Efficient stone tool kits and extraordinary murals painted on cave walls far beyond the reach of daylight bespeak the economic and intellectual attainments of these hardy cave dwellers. Peoples of the New World proved no less willing to use such natural havens. For geological reasons, the Southwest is particularly well endowed with rock shelters, of which thousands were occupied at one time or another.

Given the proclivity of humans to exploit natural shelters and the abundance of these features in the Southwest, some fairly stringent limits must be imposed to prevent this discussion from ramifying indefinitely. Restricting the focus to structures actually built in natural rock shelters eliminates the numerous shelters and rooms built against translocated objects such as slump boulders. Therefore, this discussion is limited to above-ground masonry or adobe buildings erected within the protective confines of natural rock shelters. Even with these constraints, we face an embarrassment of riches.

A symposium at the 1978 Annual Meeting of the Society for American Archaeology in Tucson brought together archaeologists and architects to consider the attributes, geographical extent, time span, and causes of cliff dwellings in the Southwest. This type of settlement was noted for the entire region from northern Utah to northern Mexico and from the Colorado River to the Pecos. Rock overhangs in extreme northeastern Utah and northwestern Colorado shelter small sites of the Fremont cultural tradition. Innumerable cliff dwellings dot the Anasazi domain on the Colorado Plateau, from the southern tip of Nevada to the Rio Grande and from Central Utah to the Little Colorado River. Less well known, but no less impressive, are the cliff dwell-

Prehistoric corn cache excavated from Antelope House, Canyon del Muerto, in 1906. Photo by Simeon Schwenberger. Courtesy, National Park Service, Hubbell Trading Post.

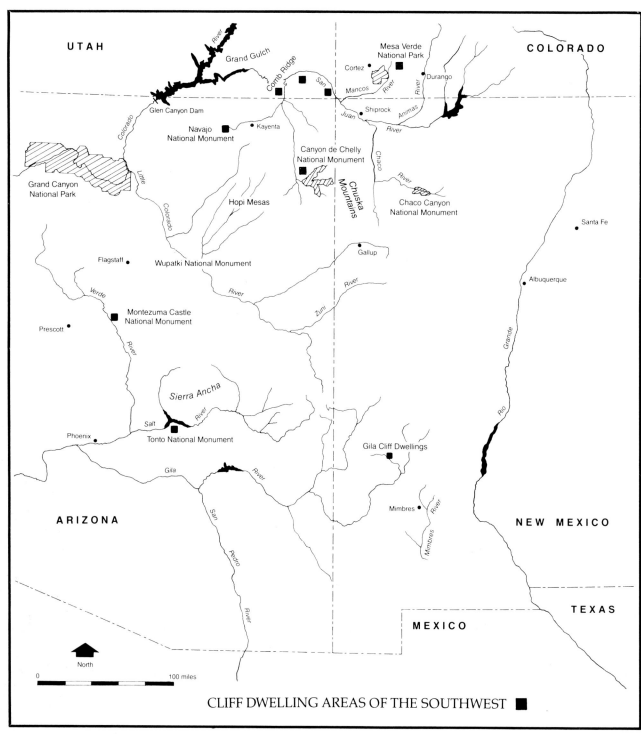

UTAH

COLORADO

Grand Gulch

Mesa Verde
National Park

Comb Ridge

Cortez

Durango

Glen Canyon Dam

Mancos

Navajo
National Monument

Kayenta

Shiprock

Animas

Juan

River

Canyon de Chelly
National Monument

Chaco

River

Grand Canyon
National Park

Little

Colorado

Hopi Mesas

Chuska
Mountains

Chaco Canyon
National Monument

Santa Fe

Flagstaff

Wupatki National Monument

Gallup

Albuquerque

Verde

River

Zuni

River

Montezuma Castle
National Monument

Prescott

Rio

Grande

Sierra Ancha

River

Salt

Phoenix

Tonto National Monument

Gila Cliff Dwellings

Gila

River

ARIZONA

San

Pedro

Mimbres

River

NEW MEXICO

Mimbres

River

TEXAS

MEXICO

North

0   100 miles

CLIFF DWELLING AREAS OF THE SOUTHWEST ■

Map by Dany Walthall

ings scattered along the precipice of the Mogollon Rim from central New Mexico to west of Flagstaff, Arizona. Deep canyons draining south from the Mogollon highlands are replete with cave sites ranging from the Gila Cliff Dwellings near Silver City, New Mexico on the east, through the cave pueblos of the rugged Sierra Ancha, to the large sheltered pueblos of the Verde River drainage. South of the Salt River are the small cave pueblos of Tonto National Monument. Farther south still, the rugged fastness of Mexico's Sierra Madre harbors hundreds of extraordinarily well-preserved, little-known cliff dwellings.

Cliff dwellings exhibit a temporal range as impressive as their geographical extent. Rock shelters were heavily used long before actual pueblos were built in them. Archaic groups of the first few millennia B.C. made extensive use of these natural shelters as did later Basketmaker II (c. A.D. 1–550), III (c. A.D. 550–850), and Pueblo I (c. A.D. 850–1000) populations. True cliff dwellings, however, emerged only sometime after A.D. 900, when people began to build surface living rooms as well as storage chambers and pithouses in rock shelters. On the Colorado Plateau, cliff dwellings are most abundant during the twelfth and thirteenth centuries, after which much of the area with suitable rock formations was abandoned as Anasazi populations concentrated in the broad Little Colorado and Rio Grande drainage basins. In the rugged Mogollon highlands and the canyons to the south, cliff dwellings persisted into the fourteenth and perhaps even fifteenth centuries. The cliff dwellings of the Sierra Madre are poorly dated but appear to have been occupied into the fourteenth century and perhaps later. Winter habitation of structures built in rock shelters by the Tarahumara Indians of northern Sonora brings the use of cliff dwellings up to the present.

Sites classified here as cliff dwellings appear to run the gamut of functions recognized for open Puebloan sites. Most appear to be habitation sites; that is, places where people resided and carried on most routine activities and other more esoteric pursuits such as religious observances. Although some archaeologists contend that cliff dwellings were used only seasonally, the majority of these sites exhibit a range of features and materials that indicates year-round use. Other rock-shelter sites appear to have served more specialized functions. A large number clearly were used primarily or solely for food storage, a practice that took advantage of the dry environment of rock shelters. A few were used principally for defense as indicated by their restricted access, defensive walls, and lack of domestic features. Fewer still, such as Fire Temple at Mesa Verde, seem to have been reserved primarily for ceremonial activities.

Architectural materials, techniques, and forms in cliff dwellings are identical to those present in open sites; however, the better preservation of the former provides a more complete picture of the architectural capabilities of the prehistoric inhabitants of the Southwest. Most cliff dwellings, like most open pueblos, are built of stone masonry laid with varying amounts of mud mortar. Masonry styles range from the elegant banded type characteristic of Chaco Canyon through the large, carefully shaped blocks arranged in even courses at Mesa Verde to virtually random agglomerations of unshaped stones set in copious quantities of mortar, such as occur at Navajo National Monument. Walls of adobe bricks and of coursed adobe also occur, notably at Inscription House in Navajo Canyon and in the Sierra Madre. Jacal walls formed from a screen of upright poles plastered with mud are particularly evident in well-preserved cliff dwellings. A cliff pueblo made almost entirely of wood reportedly exists in a remote canyon in southeastern Utah.

Jacal walls, Kiet Siel ruins, ca. 1920. Courtesy, Museum of New Mexico (neg. no. 66769).

Two additional facts relevant to the use of cliff-sheltered sites emerged from the Tucson symposium. First, rock shelters were utilized whenever the localities in which they occur were occupied by human groups. Second, the number of people residing in cliff dwellings never approached the number living in open sites. By and large, rock shelters, when available, seemed to have served as alternative loci for the same sorts of activities that took place in the open pueblos. In most respects, except degree of protection from the elements, cliff dwellings were equivalent to local open sites. Thus, while their degree of preservation makes cliff dwellings exceptional to us, they apparently were not particularly special to the people who built and lived in them.

The Cliff Dwellings of Canyon de Chelly and Tsegi Canyon

Of the innumerable cliff dwellings scattered across the Southwest, the most widely known are those in Mesa Verde National Park in southwestern Colorado and Canyon de Chelly and Navajo national monuments in northeastern Arizona. The two Arizona monuments, which are the focus of this issue of *Exploration*, share a number of features but are quite different in other ways. The names of the canyons, Chelly and Tsegi, represent, respectively, Hispanicized and Anglicized versions of the same Navajo word. *Tséyi'*, which literally translated means "among the rocks," is a common Navajo appellation for canyons. Both monuments feature some of the most spectacular canyon scenery in the United States. But differences in geology and erosion have created quite different appearances in the two canyon systems.

Cut into the dense, crossbedded de Chelly sandstone of Permian age, Canyon de Chelly and its tributary Canyon del Muerto are characterized by dark, confining walls that rise vertically from the narrow canyon floor. Created by the incision of a meandering stream, these canyons wind back and forth in a labyrinthine series of recurving loops, along which the view is restricted to short stretches of canyon and narrow slices of sky. In contrast, Tsegi Canyon is eroded into a series of Triassic-Jurassic rock layers—the crossbedded Lukachukai member of the Wingate sandstone, the flatbedded Kayenta formation, and the crossbedded Navajo sandstone—which are of differing

degrees of resistance to erosion. As a result the Tsegi has a more open aspect, presenting a broad, stepped profile rather than a straight vertical cross section. Tsegi Canyon also lacks the extreme sinuosity of Canyon de Chelly, and broad canyon vistas are common.

Erosion of the de Chelly sandstone has formed sheer, curtainlike cliffs embellished with an intricate tracery of natural bedding planes, mineral stains, and the swirling curves of great conchoidal fractures that have riven the solid rock. The less resistant Wingate and Navajo sandstones of Tsegi Canyon, folded and jointed by contortions of the earth's crust, form fantastic rounded domes and minarets, soaring buttresses, and fluted columns.

Differential erosion also creates important distinctions between the two canyon systems in the locations and configurations of rock shelters. The dense de Chelly sandstone erodes to produce moderately large, arch-shaped alcoves and, at the contact between the sandstone's two subunits, low, linear overhangs. Shelters ranging from the base of the cliffs to just below the canyon rim were occupied prehistorically. All the rock units in Tsegi Canyon offer rock shelters. Most of the occupied alcoves, however, are in the massive Navajo sandstone, which forms the rimrock of the canyon. Weathering along the contact between the crossbedded Navajo sandstone and the underlying, flatbedded Kayenta formation produces hemispherical rock shelters, some of

Aerial views of Tsegi Canyon and Canyon de Chelly. Photos by Paul Logsdon, 1985.

Antelope House, Canyon del Muerto.
Photo by Karl Kernberger, ca. 1977.

which are enormous. Smaller, almond-shaped alcoves develop from less resistant pockets in the Navajo sandstone. Although occupied rock shelters range from the bottom of the canyon to just below the rim, most Tsegi Canyon cliff dwellings are situated in alcoves at the base of the Navajo sandstone.

The Tsegi and de Chelly cliff dwellings share an important attribute in contradistinction to those of Mesa Verde. The former are oriented primarily toward the canyon bottoms, while the latter are oriented principally toward the mesa tops. At Mesa Verde, the narrow canyon bottoms possess too little arable land to have supported even a fraction of the cliff dwellings' population. Mesa-top water and soil control devices confirm the Mesa Verdeans' focus on the uplands. In Canyon de Chelly and, especially, in Tsegi Canyon, arable land is concentrated in the alluvial, well-watered, and relatively broad canyon floors. Upland soils in these areas are sparser and less productive than those at Mesa Verde, and the paucity of upland agricultural features attests to the canyon orientation of these groups. Thus, primary access to rock shelters was from above at Mesa Verde and from below in the two canyon systems.

Rock shelters in both canyon systems were used throughout most of the prehistoric occupation in these localities. The few Paleoindian big game hunters who wandered into the area apparently ignored the rock shelters, perhaps because the game animals on which they depended avoided the confined canyons in favor of the more open, grassier valleys. Similarly, little evidence of the use of the rock shelters by Archaic period hunters and gatherers has surfaced. In both canyons, intensive exploitation of rock shelters began in the Basketmaker II period when local populations first adopted a food-producing (farming) way of life. Basketmaker II sites in Canyons de Chelly and del Muerto range from small overhangs with a few storage cists to huge alcoves, such as Mummy Cave, that were inhabited for centuries and have produced a rich variety of Basketmaker II structures, artifacts, and burials. Apart from Woodchuck Cave, which was mainly a locus for human interments, major Basketmaker II sites have yet to be investigated in Tsegi Canyon. In the nearby canyon of Kin Biko, however, the prosaically named Caves 1 and 2 yielded abundant Basketmaker II perishable material and burials.

After A.D. 550, Basketmaker III peoples, who are distinguished archaeologically from Basketmaker II by the presence of ceramics and the bow and arrow, built pithouses and storage facilities in the rock shelters of both canyons. Tsé Yaa Tsoh, an immense alcove in Canyon del Muerto, sheltered a sizable Basketmaker III pithouse village. Alcoves in tributaries of the Tsegi system, such as Nagashi Bikin in Dogoszhi Biko and Cave 1 in Bubbling Springs Canyon, were loci of smaller agglomerations of Basketmaker III pithouses. Conventional wisdom holds that Pueblo I peoples eschewed rock shelters. Nevertheless, Mummy Cave 2 in Canyon del Muerto and Twin Caves and Nagashi Bikin in Dogoszhi Biko produced Pueblo I structures and trash.

Throughout the Southwest, the period from A.D. 1000–1200 was one in which rock shelters were relatively neglected as places of full-time habitation. Canyon de Chelly and the Tsegi conform to this generalization in that occupation of rock shelters declined at this time; however, it did not cease entirely. The lower White House Ruin and Antelope House in Canyon de Chelly and NA2543 and Lenaki in the Tsegi are sheltered sites occupied during this interval. Still, the A.D. 1200–1250 period probably marks the nadir of rock shelter habitation in both canyons. In the Tsegi this phenomenon relates mainly to the general disuse of the canyon at this time. Only Hostile House, a small cliff dwelling in the gap between Kiet Siel Canyon and the main Tsegi dates to this interval. This defensive site may represent the cautious beginning of a major reoccupation of the Tsegi between A.D. 1250 and 1300.

Both canyon systems were loci of major cliff dwelling construction during late Pueblo III times (A.D. 1250–1300). In Canyon del Muerto, Mesa Verdean immigrants built the Mummy Cave Pueblo with its painted kivas, massive masonry walls, and soaring rectangular tower. In de Chelly, the upper ruin at White House was added to the alcove above the lower ruin. To the south, the dioramalike Three Turkey House was built in a tributary of Nazlini Canyon. North of Canyon de Chelly, Poncho House with its central rectangular tower was erected in a shelter overlooking a broad sweep of Chinle Wash. Tsegi Canyon was the scene of a major population influx during this period. More than a score of cliff dwellings, ranging in size from only a few rooms to more than a hundred chambers, were built wherever suitable rock shelters existed. In the main canyon are Swallow's Nest; Scaffold House, with its magnificent wooden platform lodged in a crevice high above the rooms; Terrace Ruin; and NA2544. The major tributary, Dogoszhi Biko, shelters Lolomaki, NA2606, Batwoman House, Twin Caves Pueblo, Nagashi Bikin, and Priestess Cave. One of the twin jewels in the crown of Navajo National Monument, Betatakin nestles in an immense, domed rock shelter located in a verdant tributary of the main canyon. Kiet Siel, so well-preserved that it seems only temporarily vacated within the last few days, occupies a deep recess in the west wall of Kiet Siel Canyon.

The late Pueblo III occupations of both canyons were short-lived because their residents soon joined their neighbors in a general exodus from the San Juan drainage. In both canyons, the latest tree-ring dates from cliff pueblos (or any other kind of site) fall in the middle 1280s, and these sites were likely left soon after construction ceased. Thus, both locales probably were completely abandoned by A.D. 1300 at the latest. Undoubtedly, their former residents moved south and east to become part of major population buildups in

Scaffold House, Tsegi Canyon system. Photo by William C. Stoughton. Courtesy National Park Service.

Nagashi Bikin, Tsegi Canyon system. Photo by Jonathan Haas, 1984.

Betatakin, Navajo National Monument. Photo by David Noble, 1976.

the Hopi Mesas area, at Zuni, and in the Rio Grande Valley. Clearly, this emigration was part of a widespread, interrelated redistribution of Pueblo populations.

Apparently substantial environmental changes combined with social organizational factors to stimulate this process. Geological and dendrochronological studies indicate that a primary episode of arroyo cutting, which would have destroyed vast areas of farmland and lowered alluvial water tables away from the ground surface, coincided with a prolonged drought at this time. The abandonment of the Tsegi area probably represented a relocation from a region of sharply diminished agricultural potential to one characterized by a much more stable land-water relationship. Whatever the precise cause, after A.D. 1300 the cliff dwellings of the Colorado Plateau stood empty in mute testimony to the lives of the people who had built, lived in, and finally deserted them.

After the abandonment of the San Juan drainage, the focus of cliff dwelling construction shifted south to the Mogollon highlands. There is no indication that these cliff sites are in any way related to those of the Tsegi or Canyon de Chelly. Rather, they seem to be independent outcomes of whatever processes induce people to erect houses in rock shelters and caves.

Well-preserved granary, Grand Gulch, Utah. Photo by David Noble, 1985.

Why Cliff Dwellings?

At present, it is difficult to specify a set of circumstances that invariably leads to the construction of cliff dwellings. In fact, the relative contribution of different causes undoubtedly varies considerably from instance to instance. It *is* possible, however, to indentify some conditions and factors that must have influenced the decision to build cliff pueblos and to examine the relevance of these factors to the thirteenth century de Chelly and Tsegi situations.

For cliff dwelling construction, suitable rock shelters must be available. Acceptable rock shelters exhibit at least a minimal overhang to provide some protection from the weather; enough of a floor, either bedrock or talus, to allow room construction; and sufficient stability to minimize the possibility of alcove roof collapse. Obviously, both Canyon de Chelly and Tsegi Canyon fulfill these conditions.

Given the necessary prior conditions, what factors might prompt a group of people to occupy a suitable rock shelter? One reason, especially in confined canyon environments, is to get one's residence off the flood plain, a desirable goal for two reasons. First, the limited arable land in the narrow canyons is too precious a resource to waste on habitation. Second, an unstable flood plain is a poor place to live because one's home is subject to flooding, burial in accumulating sediments, waterlogging by alluvial ground water, and destruction by erosion. In some canyon localities, as at Kiet Siel, a rock shelter is virtually the only alternative to construction on the flood plain. In many other localities, however, suitable alternatives to rock shelters (such as ridges, buttes, and talus slopes) are abundant, so avoidance of the canyon floor is not a satisfactory explanation of the occurrence of cliff dwellings.

Another obvious reason for choosing a rock shelter over other suitable building sites is protection from the elements. Residents of alcoves are spared the inconvenience of retreating indoors during rain storms and do not have to contend with snow. This may seem a somewhat inconsequential motive

White House, Canyon de Chelly. Photo by David Noble, 1982.

11

Inscription House, Navajo National Monument. Photo by David Noble, 1976.

for avoiding more conveniently located open sites. However, anyone who has experienced the enormous destructive power of a southwestern summer convectional storm or the prolonged assault of a winter frontal storm can appreciate this desire. Rock shelters also modulate fluctuations in temperature. The rock absorbs the heat of the day and radiates it back at night, thus mitigating extremes of heat and cold. That temperature control was an issue in the choice of rock shelters is shown by a tendency of cliff dwellings to occur in east- and south-facing alcoves that are shaded in the summer and exposed to the rays of the low winter sun. Thus protection from the weather is a major benefit of living in rock shelters and probably was a primary consideration to peoples who do not construct substantial houses. However, alone it seems a somewhat inadequate explanation of rock-shelter occupation by people capable of building sturdy, fairly impervious masonry structures.

A factor often neglected in explanations of cliff dwellings is the ideal conditions for food storage found in rock shelters, no small consideration to farmers dependent on stored food reserves to survive the winter. The desiccation that has preserved these cliff sites also protected stored food from the mildew, mold, and rot that would have been endemic in open sites exposed to precipitation and temperature extremes. Furthermore, granaries constructed on the bedrock floors of alcoves can be sealed much more effectively against the depredations of vermin and insects than can such chambers in open sites, where burrowing animals and insects are a constant threat. It is surely no accident that initial intensive utilization of rock shelters in both canyon systems coincided with the adoption of farming. Facilities for storing perishable materials are the most abundant Basketmaker II structures found in rock shelters. The emphasis on food storage continues through the Pueblo III period. Isolated alcove granaries and small cliff dwellings composed entirely of storage chambers are common—often in direct association with nearby open sites or larger cliff pueblos. Many residential cliff dwellings exhibit a higher ratio of storerooms to living rooms than do contemporaneous open sites. Concern for food preservation probably was a major factor in the selection of rock shelters over otherwise acceptable open locations, even those more conveniently situated relative to farmland and trails.

A strong association between cliff dwellings and springs in Tsegi Canyon indicates that drinking water was another important factor in the decision to occupy a rock shelter rather than an open site and in the choice of one alcove over another. The relationship between springs and cliff dwellings is less strong in Canyon de Chelly, suggesting that drinking water may not have been so important a consideration in the choice of suitable alcoves. However, rock shelters in de Chelly tend to be close to the stream, which may have been the primary source of water.

Some attributes of cliff dwellings suggest that they may have served defensive purposes, either as fortified villages or as refuges in time of strife. Remoteness and difficulty of access are two relevant traits. Many cliff dwellings are located in branch canyons some distance from both the arable land and the communication routes of the main stems. Similarly, many can be reached only after strenuous hikes and precarious scrambles up steep slopes. Others are at present impossible to enter without technical mountain climbing gear and procedures. Three factors should be remembered in considering this degree of inaccessibility, however. First, isolation and inaccessibility are aspects of the rock shelters rather than of the villages themselves. Once the decision had been made to live in a cliff dwelling, its inhabitants were constrained to build where the rock shelters occurred and to put up with the limitations of the selected alcoves. Second, the Anasazi were apparently inured to heavy physical exertion and less intimidated by narrow ledges and vertiginous heights than are we. Finally, the Anasazi were quite capable of fashioning ladders that would have eased the way into many of the most daunting ledges and alcoves.

Difficulty of access notwithstanding, rock shelters probably are not especially good defensive positions. Many cliff dwellings have such limited fields of view that an enemy could get quite close before being discovered. Once assaulted, the defenders of a cliff dwelling are trapped, with their only escape route occupied by the attackers. Moreover, the defenders' offensive efforts are similarly limited to the direction in which the enemy forces are concentrated. An isolated eminence with controllable access offers far better defensive prospects than does a rock shelter. Field of view is unimpeded, potential escape routes are multiplied, and a more flexible defense can be mounted, either on a broad front or at the point of attack. Suitable eminences abound in both canyon systems but were not used for defensive purposes.

The defensive shortcomings of rock shelters could have been partially rectified by the construction of defensive works such as walls, bastions, offset entryways, and loopholes. Such features are rare in both Canyon de Chelly and Tsegi Canyon cliff dwellings. In fact, the few sites with unequivocal defensive features, such as Hostile House in the Tsegi, stand out in sharp contrast to the majority of cliff dwellings, which lack such features. Intentional restriction of access by walls, formal entries, and the positioning of rooms is commonplace but seems intended more to channel foot traffic through the pueblos rather than for defensive reasons. In Tsegi Canyon, the springs were not protected from capture, a potentially serious defensive oversight. Thus, while most cliff dwellings are undeniably defendable, there is little evidence to suggest that they were primarily defensive in nature.

It has been suggested that concealment was a major defensive advantage of cliff dwellings and that rock shelters served as hideaways from potential foes. Many cliff dwellings *are* tucked away in obscure recesses and screened by dense vegetation. Just as many, however, stand in plain sight, and a large number of well-hidden alcoves are devoid of occupation. In several instances, attention was purposefully directed to cliff dwellings. The gleaming facade of White House is clearly visible from the floor and opposite rim of Canyon de Chelly. The central unit and tower of Mummy Cave dominate a long stretch of Canyon del Muerto and are visible from many points on the canyon rim. Kiet Siel in the Tsegi and the prominent tower of a cliff dwelling in nearby Long House Valley can be seen from great distances. Conspicuous petroglyphs direct attention to Betatakin and Batwoman House in Tsegi Canyon. Given these facts, concealment seems not to have been an important determinant of the existence and location of cliff dwellings.

Apparently, a complex set of variables governed the occurrence and distribution of cliff dwellings in Canyon de Chelly and Tsegi Canyon. The reservation of canyon floors for agricultural pursuits, the storage potential of dry rock shelters, the presence of potable water, protection from the elements, and limited defensive advantages seem to have been the most important considerations in both areas. Whatever the specific motivations, in building their pueblos in the preservative ambiance of dry rock shelters, the prehistoric residents of Canyon de Chelly and Tsegi Canyon left a priceless memorial to a way of life that flourished there 700 years ago. This legacy can be experienced by all who visit Navajo and Canyon de Chelly national monuments, where these ruins are carefully conserved for the edification of this and future generations.

Kiet Siel, Navajo National Monument. Photo by David Noble, 1985.

Jeffrey Dean is an archaeologist and professor at the University of Arizona's Laboratory of Tree Ring Research.

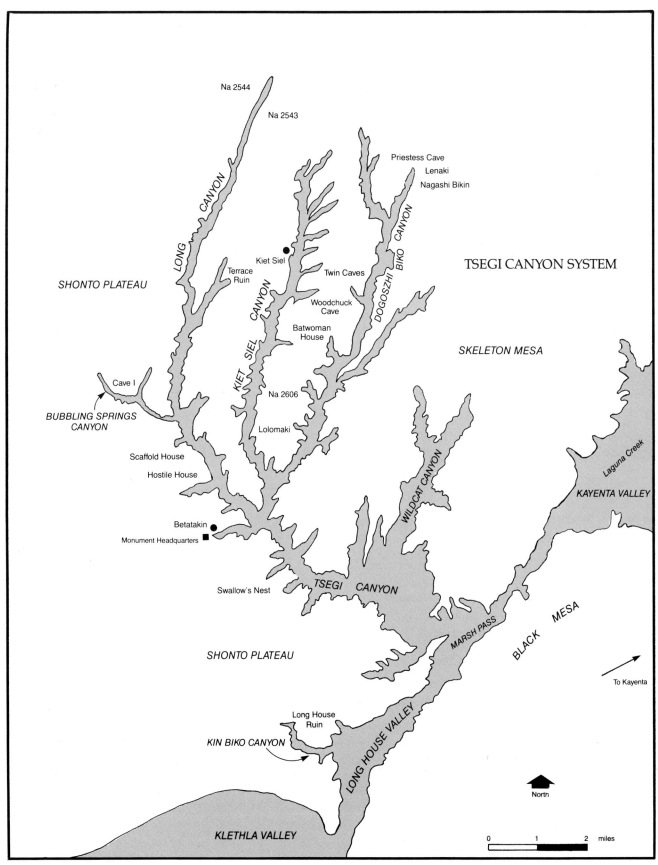

Na 2544

Na 2543

Priestess Cave

Lenaki

Nagashi Bikin

LONG CANYON

Kiet Siel

SHONTO PLATEAU

Terrace Ruin

Twin Caves

KIET SIEL CANYON

DOGOSZHI BIKO CANYON

TSEGI CANYON SYSTEM

Woodchuck Cave

Batwoman House

SKELETON MESA

Cave I

Na 2606

BUBBLING SPRINGS CANYON

Lolomaki

Laguna Creek

KAYENTA VALLEY

Scaffold House

Hostile House

WILDCAT CANYON

Betatakin

Monument Headquarters

Swallow's Nest

TSEGI CANYON

BLACK MESA

MARSH PASS

SHONTO PLATEAU

To Kayenta

Long House Ruin

KIN BIKO CANYON

LONG HOUSE VALLEY

North

0   1   2   miles

KLETHLA VALLEY

Map by Dany Walthall

Sosi Black-on-white jar, ca. A.D. 1170-1200. Photo by Pete Bennett. Courtesy, National Park Service, Navajo National Monument.

The Evolution of the Kayenta Anasazi

By Jonathan Haas

O N MY FIRST VISIT to Navajo National Monument, I led a group of university students on an archaeological field trip. While I was ready to give a classroom lecture on the cliff dwelling ruins of Betatakin and Kiet Siel, I was not prepared for the striking character of the ruins themselves. As I hiked down the trail and rounded the last outcrop for my first look at Betatakin, I was awed by the sight before me. Spread across the back of an enormous alcove, the ruins were magnificent. The fact that I was with a group of perhaps fifteen other people led by a Park Service ranger did nothing to lessen my feeling of discovery. The experience was like taking a step back in time—an archaeologist's ultimate dream.

Later a hike to Kiet Siel intensified the impression of stepping back into the past. The long trail through the deep and majestic canyons served as a transition from the modern world of high technology to the ancient one of cut stone and handmade ceramics. Looking up into the village of more than one hundred fifty rooms nestled in the back of the large shelter, I felt as if the people were simply out in their fields for the day and would return shortly to start their fires for the evening meal.

As a result of those first enchanting visits to the ruins of Navajo National Monument, I resolved to return to learn more about the people, the Kayenta Anasazi, who left behind their hauntingly beautiful cliff dwellings. Several years later I had the opportunity to come back to conduct fieldwork in the region. My focus was the history and society of the Kayenta people on a broad, regional level. I wanted to learn, for example, about the relationships between the residents of Betatakin and Kiet Siel and the people who lived in villages located in the valleys and on the mesas surrounding the canyon system.

How and why did the culture change from the relatively simple life of nomadic hunters and gatherers to the more complex life of settled village farmers? What factors ultimately led the people to gather into large, protected villages in the canyons and elsewhere during the fifty years just prior to abandonment in 1300? In conducting the field research necessary to address these questions, I have come to know and appreciate even more the beauty of northeastern Arizona. Fortunately I have been able to camp each year at Navajo National

Monument, an experience that has greatly enhanced the pleasure of working in this region.

The Kayenta Anasazi occupied a dramatic land of wide open valleys, broad mesas, and deep, majestic canyons. Their homeland extended west to the Grand Canyon, east to the Chuska Mountains, north to Glen Canyon and the Colorado River, and south to the Hopi Mesas (see map, page 4). A remarkable similarity existed among the scattered groups of Kayenta people who inhabited this wide region of diverse environments. Settlement patterns, ceramic design styles, chipped stone artifacts, and other attributes of the culture are very much alike from one area to the next. This cultural homogeneity offers archaeologists the first clue as to the nature of social relations among the Kayenta Anasazi.

Early Nomads

We do not know precisely when the first Native Americans entered the wide territory of northeastern Arizona, though there are indications that hunters stalked game in the area as long as 10,000 or more years ago. By roughly 5000 B.C., small, scattered bands of nomadic hunters and gatherers occupied the area. These people shared a lifestyle quite similar to that of other people throughout the northern Southwest. The early nomads moved frequently in a "seasonal round," taking advantage of various wild food resources as they became ready for harvest at different times of the year. They lived in temporary brush shelters or lean-tos and had no knowledge of pottery making.

The archaeological sites they left behind usually contain light scatters of broken and chipped stone, arrowheads or spearpoints, and grinding stones for processing wild seeds and other foodstuffs. The only identifiable household features we find at these sites are

Basketmaker II pithouse. Sketch by Rob Dunlavey. © 1984 Board of Trustees, Southern Illinois University.

hearths and possible work surfaces or remnants of the temporary shelters. A few particularly favorable locales, such as caves or rock shelters, were occupied repeatedly, and at these places are deep layered deposits of trash and debris spanning centuries, or even millennia.

This nomadic lifestyle lasted for nearly 5,000 years in northeastern Arizona. The culture and artifacts left by the people who lived during this time are virtually indistinguishable from those of their neighbors in other parts of the northern Southwest. In fact, aside from indications of the use of local stone and mineral sources, we find that a distinct Kayenta "culture" does not really become evident in the archaeological record until much later, about A.D. 500.

The first step in the emergence of locally distinct cultures, including the Kayenta, occurred when people assumed a less nomadic lifestyle. This important change developed as they began to cultivate their own food supply rather than to rely solely on a harvest of wild plants.

Horticulture and Sedentism

Domesticated maize (corn) first played a significant role in the Kayenta diet around 500 B.C., although it may have been introduced into the area before that time. Over the course of the next 1,000 years, maize became increasingly important in the diet, and this plant had a profound impact on the local culture.

By A.D. 500, the people of northeastern Arizona had abandoned their nomadic way of life to settle in semi-permanent villages. Maize fields require tending through the planting and growing seasons, of course, and thus they gave the farmer a reason for staying in one place for a good part of the year. Furthermore, since maize can be effectively stored for consumption throughout the year, the people no longer needed to move constantly in search of seasonal food sources. While the Kayenta may possibly have moved each year from summer to winter settlements, the relative permanence of this agricultural lifestyle resulted in new technologies and much more substantial housing.

The year A.D. 500 marks the beginning of the Basketmaker III period in northeastern Arizona.* At this time, the people were living in small villages composed of three or four to twenty or more pithouse-type structures. The Basketmakers cultivated maize and some beans and squash, and to supplement their diet, they continued to collect and eat wild resources such as piñon nuts and amaranth.

Although they may have kept domesticated turkeys, their main meat sources were rabbits, other small rodents, deer, and antelope. Ceramics make their first appearance around A.D. 600, and the initial types are basic, fairly nondescript graywares. These early cer-

Lino Black-on-gray jar. © 1985, Board of Trustees, Southern Illinois University.

amics, used for cooking, holding water, and storing produce, provide evidence of the social interactions in northeastern Arizona.

The two ceramic types found in the Kayenta area in the early Basketmaker III period are Lino Gray and Lino Black-on-gray. These are also found throughout much of the Anasazi region. This widespread distribution of common pottery types indicates that the various culture groups (Kayenta, Mesa Verde, Chaco, and so on) had not yet clearly emerged as distinct local societies. There was an unbounded social network between neighboring villages, which extended across northern Arizona and New Mexico and into southern Utah.

On the basis of modern ethnographic studies, we can assume that the people in the ancient Anasazi villages would have traded with one another, intermarried, and shared in common religious ceremonies. Family ties would have been the closest relationships between villages within this network. With no cultural or political boundaries to inhibit interaction between communities,

ceramic design styles as well as other customs would have flowed freely from one part of the Anasazi region to the next.

Another clue to social interaction during Basketmaker times exists in a few sites with large circular public structures, which may have been either kivas or dance arenas. These rooms are partially subterranean and up to ten meters across. While we do not know what went on inside, the size of the structures and their presence at only a few of the sites indicate that they were most likely centers for some kind of multivillage ceremonies. Thus, while no local cultural or "ethnic" differences manifest in the archaeological record during the Basketmaker period, we do have signs of increased interaction between communities on the local level.

The Pueblo Period

Pueblo I, A.D. 700–900

Beginning about A.D. 700, with the onset of the Pueblo period, there were significant shifts in community organization, demography, and material culture in the Kayenta area. Such changes also occurred in other parts of the Southwest during this time. Simultaneously substantive differences began to arise between the various culture groups in the Anasazi region. In northeastern Arizona, the people continued to live in pithouses, but they also began building above-ground masonry storerooms. Their villages, while small, were more formally laid out than during Basketmaker times.

A typical early Pueblo site comprises a row of pithouses fronting a line of masonry storerooms. The kivas were much smaller than the large communal structures of the Basketmakers, suggesting less formal interaction between villages. This pattern, coupled with the more formal layout of the villages, points to tighter social integration at the individual village level. The village, then, is the primary social unit during the early Pueblo I period.

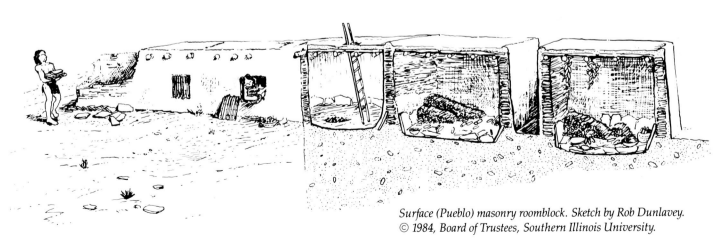

Surface (Pueblo) masonry roomblock. Sketch by Rob Dunlavey. © 1984, Board of Trustees, Southern Illinois University.

17

On a regional level, the Kayenta Anasazi were not yet fully distinct from neighboring peoples. The dominant pottery decoration, found on Kana'a Black-on-white, also occurs at that time throughout the northern Southwest. Interestingly, in the Kayenta region, Kana'a and remnant Lino Black-on-gray are the only decorated types of pottery, although elsewhere locally distinct pottery types occur along with Kana'a. In Chaco, for example, Kana'a is found with local types such as Escavada Black-on-white.

The architectural pattern and village layout found in the Kayenta region are also shared throughout most of the Anasazi region. As in the earlier Basketmaker period, therefore, distinctive culture groups recognized in later periods have not yet fully coalesced. There is, so to speak, a "generic" Anasazi culture continuing through this Pueblo I period. This culture is distinct from the other major culture groups of the Southwest, such as the Hohokam and the Mogollon, but internally, few clear distinctions exist between Anasazi subgroups.

Pueblo II, A.D. 900–1100
In the Pueblo II period, the Anasazi population grew, and distinctive local subcultures emerged. This development can be seen in the style of homes and kivas as well as in tool types and also particularly in ceramic designs. By this time, the Kayenta people had moved from pithouses to surface dwellings with stone masonry walls. It should be mentioned, however, that while the pueblo was the dominant house form after A.D. 900, the pithouse was used in some villages until the time of abandonment. The shift from pithouse to pueblo can largely be attributed to a growing need for bigger and more secure storage facilities and for additional workspace in which to process stored foods.

Left to right: Kana-a Black-on-white pitcher; Black Mesa Black-on-white bowl; Sosi Black-on-white jar. © 1985, Board of Trustees, Southern Illinois University.

Some variety in village layout is found during the Pueblo II period: a mix of pithouses and surface rooms of masonry and jacal (a hut with a thatched roof and walls of sticks covered with mud). However, by far the most common type of site consists of one or two kivas situated in front of a simple arrangement of surface rooms. These communities housed an average of two to five families and were widely dispersed across the landscape. Often they occur in locations not heavily used in earlier periods.

Apparently this was a time of many people but small communities, when the Kayenta were exploiting the full range of their vast environment. The uniformity and distinctness of the decorated pottery of the period also indicate that the Kayenta people were becoming separate from their neighbors but interacting more among themselves.

The emergent Kayenta ceramics are among the most beautiful and technically fine ever produced in the Southwest. From the simplicity of Black Mesa Black-on-white to the stark but stunning contrasts of Sosi Black-on-white and Dogozhi Black-on-white, the Kayenta people's pottery is easily distinguishable from the decorated wares of their neighbors.

Within a given pottery type, pots and sherds found in one part of the Kayenta region are indistinguishable from those found in all other parts. Thus Dogozhi found at Navajo Mountain looks like Dogozhi found on Black Mesa fifty miles to the south. Sosi sherds picked up on Cummings Mesa are essentially the same as Sosi sherds from Long House Valley.

Dogoszhi Black-on-white jar. © 1973, Board of Trustees, Southern Illinois University.

There are two possible explanations for this homogeneity of design styles: either there were common centers where much of the decorated pottery was produced, or individual potters in all the villages were making very similar pottery. There are positive indications for each argument in the archaeological record. Both alternatives indicate significantly increased social interaction within the Kayenta region and decreased, or altered, relations between the Kayenta people and people in neighboring areas. In other words, for the first time, a distinct culture group is clearly identifiable in the archaeological record.

The Kayenta continued to trade manufactured goods and exploit natural resources with their neighbors. For example, at Mesa Verde, Chaco, and south near today's Wupatki National Monument, archaeologists frequently find imported Kayenta pottery mixed in with the local wares. Within the Kayenta region are found imported turquoise, obsidian, and other resources not found locally, although one finds almost no imported pottery from outside cultures. It is impossible to determine from available evidence whether the Kayenta constituted an ethnically distinct and socially bounded unit such as a "tribe" at this time; however, the ceramics as well as other definitive traits clearly indicate that by Pueblo II times, a discrete network of social relationships united the Kayenta people and set them apart from other groups in the northern Southwest.

Pueblo III, A.D. 1100–1300

In the following Pueblo III period, major changes took place in the social development of the Kayenta Anasazi. To illustrate what occurred in the twelfth and thirteenth centuries, I would like to focus on one location, Long House Valley and neighboring areas to the east and west.

Long House Valley is located immediately to the south of Navajo National Monument, just outside the Tsegi Canyon system of Betatakin and Kiet Siel. This relatively small valley, central within the Kayenta region, has been the focus of much archaeological research over the past fifteen years. Long House provides a microcosm of the Kayenta culture of Pueblo III times.

On the way to the Monument, U.S. 160 passes through Long House Valley where half a dozen Navajo hogans are visible from the road along with small fields of corn and beans, and herds of cattle, sheep, and horses grazing on low shrubs. A hike through the valley in A.D. 1100 would have revealed a strikingly different landscape. In place of the few hogans would be many small pueblos spread widely across the valley's floor and sides. Other than the fact that some had kivas and others did not, few differences existed between these pueblos. Each served as the residence of one to three families, and each would have been surrounded by extensive fields of corn, beans, and squash. Besides a few turkeys and the inevitable yapping dogs, no domesticated animals would have appeared. Inside the houses, the beautiful Sosi and Dogozhi Black-on-white pottery would be in use, along with a variety of "orangewares" with black and red designs painted on an orange background.

This picture started to change around A.D. 1150, when a broad shift in the weather patterns of northern Arizona began. This shift introduced new hardships for the Kayenta people. The changes included a gradual decrease in annual precipitation, periodic droughts, a lowering of the water table, and increasing soil erosion.

In Long House Valley, the decreased precipitation and lower water table reduced the available arable land in the southern half of the valley and resulted in a population concentration in the northern half. The pueblos moved closer together and remained small, although a few larger communities of twenty-five to forty rooms (five to ten families) appeared on the scene for the first time.

It is unclear exactly why these larger communities were formed, but their very presence is indicative of closer social ties and increased solidarity between families. Outside Long House Valley to the east and west, a similar clustering of people occurred around shrinking plots of arable land. To the south, up on Black Mesa, an area always marginal for rainfall farming, the climatic changes were too much for the people. The mesa was abandoned at 1150.

Long House Valley. Photo by Jonathan Haas, 1984.

Across the Kayenta territory, the people apparently reacted to the drought, lower water tables, and loss of land through erosion by moving together around the remaining arable land and by uniting into larger villages. No overt signs exist of any form of competition or conflict either internally within Long House Valley or between Long House residents and their neighbors. The environment did not let up, however, and the people were faced with even greater hardships, more drought, and less arable land.

This pattern reached its peak in the latter half of the thirteenth century, with a major drought in the 1260s, and the maximum loss of land to arroyo-cutting erosion. The impact of these climatic problems is perhaps best revealed in the skeletal remains from this time. They indicate an increase in child mortality, and a broad rise in health ailments resulting from malnutrition and poor diet.

At A.D. 1250, in response to growing environmental pressures and high population densities, dramatic changes took place within the Kayenta region. These changes are indicated by architecture and artifacts and apparently affected the very nature of social relations. Villages grew tenfold, the number of kivas proliferated, and many new styles of pottery appeared. Indications exist of much closer cooperation between villages; broad alliances between valleys; and for the first time, evidence of some form of internal conflict or warfare arising in the later part of the thirteenth century.

In Long House Valley, we see the appearance of a new settlement pattern at A.D. 1250. All the sites were grouped into one of five discrete settlement "clusters" in the northern half of the valley, and two clearly different types of villages emerge. Within each village cluster

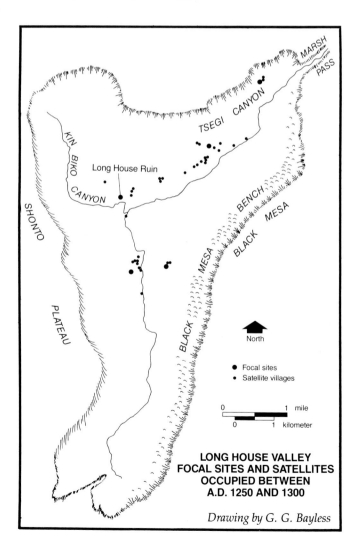

**LONG HOUSE VALLEY
FOCAL SITES AND SATELLITES
OCCUPIED BETWEEN
A.D. 1250 AND 1300**

Drawing by G. G. Bayless

20

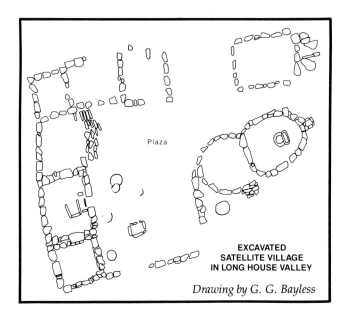

EXCAVATED
SATELLITE VILLAGE
IN LONG HOUSE VALLEY

Drawing by G. G. Bayless

were two to twelve "satellite" sites of 2–30 rooms, all surrounding a much larger "focal" site of 75–400 rooms. These focal pueblos were further distinguished from the satellite villages by the presence of open plaza areas; reservoirs for collecting and storing water; and unusual long, open room blocks, which were often two stories high and made with unique and very fine stone masonry.

All five of these focal sites were strategically placed in two ways: first, they were located on steep hilltops or prominences in defensible positions; and second, a visual link existed between each of them (i.e., you could see from each one to all the others). The placement of these focal sites points to patterns of both conflict and alliance in Long House Valley and surrounding areas.

Either conflict or the threat of conflict is indicated by the deliberate selection of site locations that can be easily defended and that overlook all major access routes into the valley. At the largest site, Long House Ruin, for example, surface remains reveal only two access corridors leading into the site. Both of these were blocked by crosswalls.

At a second location, the focal site and its satellites are perched on top of an isolated 600-foot-high sandstone cliff, overlooking the pass leading into the valley from the north. This site is only accessible by climbing a steep talus slope and then a vertical 15-foot ascent up steps and hand and toe holds through a narrow crack in the cliff. (Three small children with rock projectiles could stand at the top of this crack and keep a horde of raiders at bay.)

No water is found on top of the cliff, although the people did build at least one reservoir to catch runoff from the bedrock. There is no arable land. Thus the inhabitants must have hiked up and down the cliff each day to tend their fields and, during much of the year, to obtain

water. A reasonable inference, then, is that they moved into such an inconvenient and inaccessible spot because they were worried about being attacked. The question arises: Where would the attackers have come from?

We can probably rule out neighboring groups in Long House Valley. The fact that all the focal sites were specifically located so as to allow visual contact and communication between them points toward friendly alliance rather than conflict at the local level. And what better reason for building such an alliance than the common need to defend the valley and its resources against outside enemies? Were those enemies then to be found in the neighboring valleys to the east and west, or further afield in southern Utah, Mesa Verde, or perhaps to the south in the vicinity of the Hopi mesas?

Clearly we cannot fully understand the pattern observed in Long House Valley without looking at what is happening in neighboring areas. Although today we do not have good data that would allow us to investigate the possibility of larger scale interregional warfare, there is information about what happened within the Kayenta region.

To the north and east in the Kayenta Valley, we find a very similar pattern of settlements, with smaller satellites clustered around much larger focal sites situated on highly defensible hilltops. Some of the Kayenta Valley

Access crack to mesa-top site. Photo by Jonathan Haas, 1984.

The ruins of a defensive pueblo perch on top of this hill in the Kayenta Valley. Photo by David Noble, 1985.

sites were actually walled, and others were so inaccessible that modern survey crews spent days determining how to reach them. Commonly, access involved climbing up a near-vertical crack in the edge of the cliff face. Clearly such positions were easy to defend and hard to attack.

As in Long House, these focal sites were visually interlocked with one another; furthermore, a recent survey showed that the visual network in the Kayenta Valley was closely linked to the Long House network. However, unlike the situation to the east, a wide gap exists between the Klethla Valley system and the one in Long House, and there is no visual link between them. The easternmost of the Klethla focal sites is more than fifteen kilometers (about nine miles) from the nearest site in Long House Valley. None of the Klethla sites can be seen from any of the Long House sites. While this pattern is by no means conclusive, it does point to the possibility that the residents of the two neighboring valleys probably were not allied with one another and, in fact, may have been enemies during this period.

Stepping back to look at the area as a whole, we can see several different kinds of social interaction going on simultaneously. At the local level, clusters of communities exist within which there was probably some division and coordination of labor, land, and resources, and possibly centralized storage in the defensible focal sites. At a level above the clusters are the interlocking valley and intervalley systems, which operated to maintain communication and probably coordinated defense between

clusters and valleys. Finally, on a regional level, we find positive indications that the residents of Long House Valley and neighboring valleys worried about the possibilities of attacks or raids from the outside, and took strong defensive steps as a result.

Given that the climatic changes of the time caused droughts and a steady loss of arable land, it is not surprising that the people took whatever steps were necessary to secure their all-important supplies of food. Nor is it unusual that under those same conditions others would have attempted to gain those vital food supplies. Overall, in the latter half of the thirteenth century, we find that the social relationships among the Kayenta people are a complex combination of cooperation and conflict. The history of Kayenta Anasazi culture comes to a close at the end of the thirteenth century, when northeastern Arizona as well as most of the northern Southwest was abandoned. Why did the Kayenta leave? This is a question for which we do not have good answers today.

The deteriorated environmental conditions, coupled with high population densities in those few areas of arable land, undoubtedly spurred the abandonment of the area. The situation was likely further aggravated by endemic raiding and warfare. However, it is highly improbable that warfare alone would have caused the people to leave their homeland.

Where the Kayenta went after they left is even less clear. It appears that at least some of them migrated to central Arizona, where Kayenta-type pottery and architecture have been found at sites occupied at the end of the thirteenth century. Elsewhere, however, no signs are to be found of a Kayenta migration in the fourteenth century. Their destination remains a mystery.

In studying the evolution of the Kayenta one comes away with a tremendous feeling of empathy and admiration. For thousands of years, the prehistoric inhabitants of northeastern Arizona successfully extracted a living out of the canyons, valleys, and mesas. They constantly adapted to highly variable climatic conditions and growing populations, and built ever-closer ties with their neighbors as they evolved from nomadic hunting and gathering bands to fully sedentary tribal farmers. When faced with true hardships imposed by a changing external environment, as they were at the beginning of the twelfth century, their first response was not competition and conflict. It was to pull together and build more cooperative social networks. As the hardships continued and worsened, the social bonds strengthened and drew the people even closer.

Only when the external conditions became extreme is there the first appearance of conflict, aggression, and warfare. Warfare was a last recourse for the Kayenta. It occurred when there was simply not enough food to feed all the people, and they were suffering from malnutrition and other dietary problems. The Kayenta thus leave behind not only a legacy of great craftsmanship and creativity, but also a record of enduring adaptation and positive cooperation. They show that war and aggression are not necessarily "natural" to the human species, but responses to the most extreme kinds of external adversity.

---

*The designation "Basketmaker," which is applied to the early horticulturalists across the northern Southwest, was first used in the Kayenta area by Alfred V. Kidder and Samuel Guernsey. The two were working in rock shelters with names such as White Dog Cave and Sunflower Cave. In those sites, they found early cultural complexes that included highly sophisticated and beautiful basketry but no pottery of any kind. Thus they applied the name "Basketmakers." For the Basketmaker era, there is no period designated "Basketmaker I." Archaeologists expected to find such an initial period when they set up the chronological sequence during work in the 1920s. However, subsequent work revealed no distinct cultural sequence that can be clearly labeled the first Basketmaker period. The author has also skipped over the Basketmaker II period here because it represents a long transition between the nomadic hunting and gathering Archaic stage and the rise of horticulture and sedentism in Basketmaker III.

Jonathan Haas, a southwestern archaeologist and Director of Programs and Research at the School of American Research, has conducted field research on prehistoric Pueblo warfare in the Tsegi Canyon system.

ANASAZI ROCK ART

in Tsegi Canyon and Canyon de Chelly

A View Behind the Image

by Polly Schaafsma

Ghost-like and other Basketmaker anthropomorphs, Canyon de Chelly. Two smaller white birds (possibly quail) are painted over a red human form. Photo by Russell Bodnar 1985.

. . .early Basketmaker life and customs, as revealed by archeology and interpreted in the light of modern Indian life, [make] an unsatisfactory picture at best. That is the weakness of archeology. It tells much of the life of the body and the work of the hands, little of the life of the spirit and the work of the mind. (Charles Avery Amsden, *Prehistoric Southwesterners from Basketmaker to Pueblo.* Southwest Museum, Los Angeles, 1949, p. 96).

THE ABOVE QUOTE from Charles Amsden, part of a detailed and sensitive synthesis of Basketmaker life, expresses his frustration with the lack of archaeological evidence concerning the spiritual life and ideologies of prehistoric peoples. Amsden likens the archaeological record to "a painting [which] can give us no more than the eye can see and the imagination conjure from its revelations." He senses that "the Basketmakers [and the Anasazi in general] were as active in mind as they obviously were in body."

Nevertheless, there are certain bits of evidence in material culture that point to various aspects of Anasazi religious practices. This evidence includes rock art. Various types of studies have shown that we can find in the imagery of rock art indications of the ideological dimension of Anasazi life. Granted, when we marshal all of the evidence available, we may only glean a glimpse of this spiritual and mental realm; however, such a glimmer of insight is much better than nothing at all.

Rock art adds a tantalizing dimension to the canyons and alcoves of the Colorado Plateau. Tsegi Canyon and Canyon de Chelly are located in the central San Juan region of the plateau, an elevated tableland dissected by deep, colorful sandstone drainages. *Tsegi*, a Navajo word meaning "within the rock," and *Chelly*, a corruption of this same word, are appropriate names for these canyons, with their vertical walls offering protected arching alcoves and rock shelters, which provide a dramatic setting for the rock art. Tsegi Canyon on Laguna Creek, a tributary of the Chinle Wash, and Canyon de Chelly on the Chinle itself, share common rock-art styles representing 1300 years of Anasazi occupation. The same styles are also found on the San Juan River itself and in nearby canyons entering the San Juan from the north, such as Grand Gulch, Slickhorn Gulch, and Butler Wash. Through the centuries this art underwent gradual and perceivable changes in style, symbolism, and meaning that paralleled changes in cultural needs and values. The styles can be dated relative to each other by various instances of superimpositions, and also on an absolute basis by their associations with habitation sites.

Various estimates place the earliest Basketmaker occupation at about A.D. 1. It lasted until around A.D. 450. The rock art of this period is characterized by pecked and/or painted representations of large anthropomorphic figures with squarish or broad-shouldered, tapering bodies and drooping hands and feet. These figures may wear necklaces and sashes, and their torsos may be dotted or divided by vertical or horizontal zigzags. Headgear, when present, is conspicuous and varied. At painted sites, handprints are often numerous around the anthropomorphs. At late Basketmaker II sites in the northern San Juan, birds are sometimes located on the heads of anthropomorphs. Zigzags or snakes, atlatls and/or spears, and medicine bags or pouches are other associated elements. Archaeologists Alfred Vincent Kidder and Samuel Guernsey, working in the Tsegi region early in this century, were the first to

Top: Basketmaker woman in white and probably a shaman carrying a wicket-shaped object. This scene seems to be related to another in the same shelter in which a reclining female is administered to by someone holding over her a similar device. Canyon de Chelly. Photo by David Noble, 1985.

Bottom: Large Basketmaker II figures superimposed by birds and a smaller bird-footed anthropomorph in red. A line of red ducks occurs at the upper right. Blue Bull Cave, Canyon del Muerto. Photo by David Noble, 1985.

Positive striped prints and a single negative handprint, all in white, on a rock shelter ceiling in Canyon de Chelly. Anasazi period unknown. Photo by David Noble, 1985.

observe that the distinctive, broad-shouldered anthropomorphic forms in the rock art were consistently found in Basketmaker II shelters.

Basketmaker rock art has roots in even earlier Colorado Plateau rock-art styles found immediately to the north. These earlier styles emphasize large, abstract anthropomorphs with supernatural attributes. The figures may represent shamans, supernaturals, or supernaturals seen by shamans. In rock art of the Barrier Canyon style, quadrupeds, birds, and snakes occur around these figures in a manner suggesting that they are spirit helpers or guides.

The early styles shed light on the significance of the Basketmaker rock art, which they influenced. Like the earlier anthropomorphic figures, the Basketmaker figures are not ordinary men. They are abstract, remote, static forms, lacking human qualities. Their elaborate headgear is another clue to their supernatural affiliations. The headdresses may consist of tall terraces of lunate elements or tall feathers. Sometimes these ele-

ments are shown projecting from the left ear as well as from the top of the head. Occasionally staring eyes and unnatural hands and feet are pictured. The latter may be three-toed and bird-like or resemble clawed bear paws, both of which suggest nonhuman affiliations. The numerous handprints, birds, and occasional snakes closely associated with these ethereal beings were mentioned above. The handprints are usually stamped near the figures, or they may be placed on their torsos or around the heads. Occasionally babies' footprints were also stamped on the rocks. The consistent association of handprints with the anthropomorphs at these Basketmaker sites suggests that they were made for some definite purpose. They may have been left as signatures of prayer requests or made in the act of obtaining power—either from the rock-art figure itself or from the place it occupied. In both cases, some kind of supernatural power associated with the human forms is implicit.

Early Anasazi paintings of avian and lively human forms, a line of triangles, dot patterns and double wavylines in red and white. A white bird-headed man appears in the lower right. Canyon del Muerto. Photo by David Noble, 1985.

Early Anasazi stick figures with large birds on their heads. Kiet Siel, Navajo National Monument. Photo by David Noble, 1985.

Bottom: Early Anasazi petroglyph of anthropomorph with bird symbolism, Marsh Pass. Photo by David Noble, 1985.

Both birds and snakes are almost universally associated with shamanistic iconography and are viewed as possessors of certain types of wisdom and specific powers. Both function as messengers to other realms. Snakes have access to the underworld and symbolize regeneration and rebirth, while birds, on the other hand, are symbols for freedom and spiritual transcendence. Magical flight in bird form is common to shamanistic traditions not only in the Southwest, but worldwide.

At some point, probably late in the Basketmaker II period, birds became very important in the iconography of the canyon rock art. These birds are most commonly depicted as rather stylized, round-bodied forms without wings but often with legs drawn at an angle to convey a sense of flight. As paintings they are often done in white with red outlines, or vice versa. The heads and necks were sometimes painted in fugitive pigment so that today these birds appear headless, although this was not originally the case. Present in great numbers from late Basketmaker II into Basketmaker III times, these birds are often readily identifiable as ducks, turkeys, and occasionally geese.

Although the symbolic import for the Basketmakers of these different species of birds is difficult to determine, their significance for the modern Pueblos is instructive. Birds in general are an extremely important element in modern Pueblo ritual and mythology, and judging from their appearance, not only in rock art, but also on ceramics, in kiva murals, and as fetishes, they have enjoyed this status continuously throughout hundreds of years of prehistory. Mobile creatures that travel swiftly, birds frequently play the role of messengers in Pueblo myths. Feathers that can float on air are analagous to thoughts, and they are associated with prayers that must travel to the spirit world, to the powers controlling the rain and clouds. Thus feathers are commonly used in constructing ritual paraphernalia such as prayer sticks.

The duck's ability to be at home everywhere, from high in the air to under the water, gives him extraordinary powers. In both Mexico and the Southwest, he is ascribed shamanistic attributes. Among the contemporary Pueblo Indians, he is thought of as a ventriloquist. He is regarded as wise because he is a great traveler and searcher, migrating with the geese and cranes to which are assigned similar powers. The duck is viewed as a keeper of myths, and like other birds he functions as a messenger. Supernaturals are said to assume duck form in their travels between this world and the spirit world. The water associations of the duck are obvious, and he can carry messages to the clouds, the sources of rain. These characteristics and abilities are not inconsistent with the representations of the ducks in ancient rock art, where he occurs near or on, or replaces the heads of, figures that may represent shamans in spirit flight.

Petroglyphs of ducks or geese in flight, Marsh Pass below Tsegi Canyon. The significance of the sequences of short lines is not known. Photo by David Noble, 1985.

The turkey, a creature of the earth (as opposed to the sky), is bound to embody a different set of symbolic concepts, although this bird, too, is found in the same set of relationships to human figures in the rock art. The turkey was domesticated by the Anasazi by A.D. 700. Its feathers were used for robes and ritual purposes at least by that time and perhaps even earlier. Among the modern Pueblo Indians, the turkey is symbolically associated with the earth, springs, streams, and mountains, which are the homes of the cloud spirits. It follows that the turkey is viewed as an intermediary between these mountain water sources and the rain clouds that form on the peaks. He is also regarded as a teacher and helper, and he is associated with the dead, who must return to earth before rising as clouds to the spiritual realm. Turkey feathers are therefore used in mortuary offerings. Prehistorically, turkey burials have been found with human burials, and the practice of wrapping the dead in turkey feather robes may have been a means of assisting the dead in their spiritual journey. No research has been done to see if the turkey-headed anthropomorphic forms in rock art occur in caves containing burial cists; if such a connection were found, the rock art would also depict this relationship.

This excursion into Pueblo ideology provides a direction for understanding the ancient paintings and petroglyphs of Tsegi Canyon and Canyon de Chelly. The importance of bird symbolism in Basketmaker ceremony and art is further emphasized by some of the artifacts retrieved from Basketmaker sites. A stuffed bird skin and a bird-headed wand with feathers and bird tails attached was found in White Dog Cave, a Basketmaker II site near Tsegi Canyon. Skin medicine pouches containing feathers have also been found at Basketmaker sites.

By the time birds became abundant in the rock art of Tsegi Canyon and Canyon de Chelly, other major changes were taking place. The strict canons of Basketmaker II painting were relaxed. The austere figures of the earlier period were gradually replaced during an efflorescence of rock art in which a variety of smaller images were painted in bi- or polychrome designs. This post-Basketmaker II period was truly the heyday of rock art in Canyon de Chelly. Individuality of expression and the portrayal of unusual figures was the name of the game. There was great experimentation with the human form, which continued to be a dominant image in quantity if not in size. It was rendered in a variety of shapes including small rectangular-, trapezoidal-, and triangular-bodied forms, stick figures in frontal poses, and stick figures in profile—any one of which might appear with a bird on its head. An occasional bird-headed figure is shown with legs bent, as if actually flying through the air. There are lines of hand-holding men and women, dancing groups, Siamese twins, and seated stick figures with headdresses or headbands, playing flutes under rainbows. Others hold huge arrows or ceremonial staffs. An occasional crane was added to the avian inventory. Bizarre insects, a few nondescript animals, and mountain sheep with open mouths are represented. According to Campbell Grant, in his book on *Canyon de Chelly: Its People and Rock Art*, this complex dates between A.D. 450 and 1100. It is less well represented in the Tsegi, although some paintings in the vicinities of Kiet Siel and Scaffold House seem to date from this period.

The flute player is prominent in the rock art of Tsegi Canyon and Canyon de Chelly after the Basketmaker II period. According to Grant, the earliest flute players in Canyon de Chelly are simple stick figures. The seated flute players under rainbows may be early images of this personage as a rain priest. Later examples in Pueblo II and III rock art are more apt to be shown reclining

and kicking their heels, or as phallic and/or hump-backed images. In his more complex manifestations, the flute player is well known as Kokopelli. He may be associated with snakes or appear in hunting scenes with mountain sheep, where he seems to function as a

Early Anasazi human figures in red and white, Canyon de Chelly. Photo by Russell Bodnar.

Above: An early Anasazi figure in red plays a white flute below a rainbow while two quadrupeds frame an ambiguous object at right. Canyon de Chelly. Photo by David Noble.

Below: Pueblo III painted textile design in white and reddish brown, Canyon de Chelly. Photo by David Noble, 1985.

flute while preparing magic locust medicine for purification rites. His association with mountain sheep gives him a special relationship to the Horn Clan at Hopi. An overriding characteristic of this fellow is his sexuality and his role in fertility rites. His hump is said to be filled with babies, as well as seeds, belts, and blankets —gifts for the maidens he seduces. Klaus Wellman, who studied the symbolism of this figure in some depth, has suggested that this little personage is a regional variant of a more comprehensive archetype, the Universal Trickster. The Trickster, present in mythologies throughout the world, embodies unprincipled, amoral forces and chaos on one hand, while on the other he becomes the creator, cultural hero, and transformer. These are universal roles that the later Pueblo Indians also dramatized as the Horned Water Serpent and clowns.

The final phase of Anasazi rock art in the central San Juan (Pueblo II – III, A.D. 1000–1300) was somewhat less flamboyant than the preceding one. Both petroglyphs and large paintings in clay were popular, and only occasionally do details seem significant. Much of this rock art is found in and around cliff dwellings and other habitation sites where it must have been an everyday public phenomenon.

Flute players still appear, and mountain sheep and hunting scenes are also typical of this late phase of canyon rock art. The practice of making handprints with

Above: A five-foot long flute player smeared in white clay dominates this painted portion of a shelter wall in the Tsegi Canyon system. The Tsegi Phase flutist is painted on top of a myriad of earlier Anasazi elements painted in pastel clays. Ancient Basketmaker men and two stirrup-shaped elements loom ghost-like behind the later figures. Photo by Karl Kernberger.

Left: Tsegi Phase mountain sheep, handprints, and large circular painting in white, Betatakin, Navajo National Monument. The latter is interpreted by the Hopi as a Fire Clan symbol. Photo by Byron Cummings, 1909. Courtesy, National Park Service.

Early Anasazi figure with supernatural qualities seemingly indicated by wavy lines that emerge from either side of his head. Four stick figures in red appear to float between the zigzags. A large shamanic form with necklace appears at the right. Canyon de Chelly. Photo by David Noble, 1985.

clay and mineral pigments persisted throughout the Anasazi occupation. Formal textile or pottery motifs, lizards and lizard-men, and rectilinear stick-figure humans are characteristic. The human figures tend to be angular and geometric, although action scenes with profile figures also occur.

Particularly notable are the large, white, circular designs painted in shelters with cliff dwellings. These prominently located paintings are not only highly visible but also bold in concept. They consist of a variety of simple patterns that sometimes utilize negative designs. Others are variations on the concentric-circle motif. The large circle painting at Betatakin contains a negative image of an anthropomorph, and arcs in red and yellow are painted at the base and on either side. The figure has been interpreted by the Hopi as a representation of Masauwu, god of the earth, guardian of the dead, and controller of fire. The painting is regarded by the Hopi as a Fire Clan symbol. A set of white handprints and a carefully painted, large white mountain sheep occur to

Stamped Anasazi handprints in red bordered above and below by broad bands in white and yellow respectively. Bubbling Spring Canyon, Tsegi drainage. Photo by David Noble, 1985.

the right. It is possible that all such large white paintings in alcoves housing cliff dwellings are emblems of the social groups who occupied the sites. Certainly the large size of these paintings and their conspicuous locations would announce this information to outsiders. Jane Young, in her research with the Zuni, found that it is considered good luck to have one's clan symbol about, and this may have been equally true in the past.

Other rock art, both in the form of petroglyphs and small paintings within these alcoves, occur on the cliff walls near roof-top work areas of family dwellings. They are usually casually made and seem incidental. One set of four white handprints in Inscription House in Navajo Canyon occurs directly above a wall that divides family living areas, and these prints may have served as a sort of boundary marker within the village.

Quadrupeds such as mountain sheep, which are present throughout all periods of Anasazi rock art, become more prevalent during Pueblo II and III. It is obvious from the earlier discussion that representations of animals are usually more than simple depictions of the natural fauna, and that they were often selected for their symbolic significance and the particular powers attributed to them. Horned animals are viewed as "powerful" almost universally, and the mountain sheep in the Southwest is no exception. The mountain sheep is important in myth, and his horns are worn as symbols of power and knowledge by Hopi priests of the Horn Society. Deer and mountain sheep are also frequently represented in hunting scenes. It is probable that this imagery was made in a ritual framework in which prayers and offerings were made to either ensure a successful hunt or to propitiate the spirits of animals already slain.

Lizards and the ambiguous forms of lizard-men are prominent themes in late Anasazi art. The lizard, like the bird and the snake, is a typically shamanistic motif, symbolizing bodily transcendence and rejuvenation. Exactly what the lizard signified to the canyon artists is not known, although the existence of a definite conceptual role in the ideology of the times is reinforced by the stone lizard-woman effigy excavated from a Pueblo III kiva at Salmon Ruin on the San Juan River near Bloomfield, New Mexico. According to Young, to contemporary Zunis petroglyphs of these figures near Zuni Pueblo represent "raw beings," "the way the Zunis looked at the time of the beginning," "before they were finished," when they had tails and webbed hands and feet.

Thirteen hundred years or so of Anasazi ideas are represented by these enigmatic graphic images on the red sandstone walls of Tsegi Canyon and Canyon de Chelly. I have touched on salient characteristics and changes through time, pointing out a few of the possible and probable implications of the rock art. The art suggests that the early occupants of these spectacular red canyons were concerned with a world of spirit powers to which they related through shamanistic specialists who had access to these realms. The "life of the spirit and the work of the mind" of the Anasazi is revealed by their graphic imagery as a complex world of symbol and metaphor. It reflects a way of relating to the environment that is somewhat unfamiliar to our "scientific" rules and biases, but one that was equally as meaningful and all-encompassing.

Polly Schaafsma is a rock art specialist and author of Indian Rock Art of the Southwest. *She is also an artist.*

The Anasazi of Canyon de Chelly
by Pat Fall

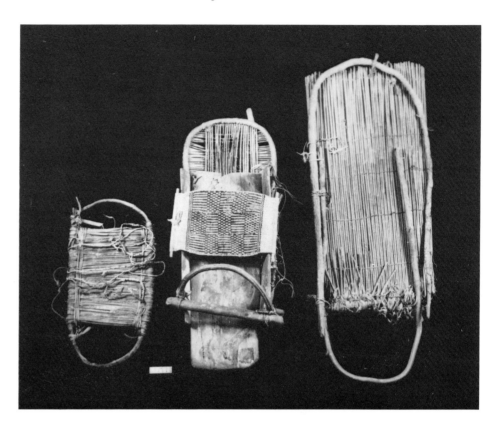

Bent cradle frames from Antelope House.
Courtesy, National Park Service.

CANYON DE CHELLY NATIONAL MONUMENT, impressive in its scenic grandeur, contains some of the most spectacular ancient homes of the Anasazi people. The red sheer-walled cliffs exposed through millennia by meandering streams and blackened with desert varnish provide a dramatic backdrop for the ruins of White House, Tse Ta'a Ruin, Ledge Ruin, Antelope House, Big Cave, Massacre Cave, and Mummy Cave. These ancient villages have fascinated and impressed archaeologists and visitors alike.

Because the Anasazi left no written or oral history, we must piece together their lives from what they discarded or left behind. The numerous dry alcoves and caves of de Chelly provided shelter to the canyon's prehistoric residents and preserved abundant evidence that they grew corn and squash; kept domestic dogs and turkeys; hunted antelope, deer, and bighorn sheep; wove fabric from cotton and hair; made blankets from rabbit fur; smoked cigarettes; were expert basket weavers; and made toys for their children.

The lure of well-preserved Basketmaker artifacts attracted Earl Morris to Canyon de Chelly in 1923. A member of the Third Bernheimer Expedition from the American Museum of Natural History, Morris was one of the first archaeologists to investigate the cliff dwellings of Canyon de Chelly. He found that for centuries the dry caves had held organic remains in an excellent state of preservation. Morris collected baskets, pottery, mummies, sandals, cordage, woven cloth, mats, furs, and wooden tools, all of which have added to our knowledge of this ancient culture.

The landscape also provides us with information. The drainages that formed the canyons originate at 9,000 feet elevation in the Chuska Mountains and pass through the expansive grasslands, steppes, and piñon-juniper woodlands that are typical of the Colorado Plateau. The plateaus, mountains, and valleys surrounding the narrow canyons offer wild game (antelope, mule deer, big horn sheep, and rabbits), piñon nuts, and wood for fuel and construction. The canyons themselves provide permanent water sources for drinking and irrigation and many edible plants unavailable on the open plateaus.

While the sheer cliffs of de Chelly and del Muerto appear to be formidable barriers to travel, del Muerto alone contains more than forty hand- and toe-hold trails that can be negotiated from canyon bottom to cliff top in about twenty minutes. These trails allowed the Anasazi of yesterday to travel between the canyons and the Defiance Plateau, and the Navajo of today make similar use of them.

Earl Morris in the driver's seat of "Old Joe" on an expedition into Canyon del Muerto, 1924. Courtesy, University of Colorado Museum.

The Earliest Inhabitants

The earliest inhabitants of the region around Canyon de Chelly led a nomadic life, hunting small game and gathering wild plants and seeds. These pre-Anasazi people, called "Archaic" by archaeologists, lived between 5500 and 200 B.C. in small scattered bands or family groups. They migrated with the seasons, followed wild plant harvests and game, and found shelter in natural or temporary shelters.

Relatively little is known about the Archaic people. Although they may have traveled through the region, stopping to gather wild food and hunt, they were never very numerous at Canyon de Chelly. The only evidence of these hunters and gatherers in the canyon is a few stone spearpoints. Several of these Archaic points were found mixed with Anasazi artifacts at Antelope House Ruin. Perhaps these spearpoints, broken or lost by their first owners, were later picked up and brought to Antelope House by the Anasazi.

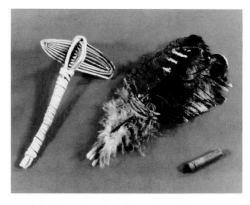

Owl fetish, feather bundle, and reed cigarette. Courtesy, National Park Service.

The Basketmakers

The first evidence we have for habitation in Canyon de Chelly was left by the earliest Anasazi, the Basketmakers. The early Basketmakers were expert basket weavers, but did not know the craft of pottery making. The Basketmakers appeared at various times across the Colorado Plateau, beginning about 200 B.C. Dates gleaned from tree-ring samples of wood found in storage bins indicate that they came to Canyon de Chelly sometime between A.D. 300 and 420.

The Basketmakers were the first people on the Colorado Plateau to develop an economy based on farming. They brought with them the knowledge of cultivating maize (corn) and squash. These crops, originally domesticated in Mexico, were staples of the Basketmaker diet. They were able to grow enough corn to produce a surplus to store for winter consumption when fresh food resources were scarce. This security of having food available throughout the year allowed the Basketmakers to settle in one place, and relieved them of the necessity of migrating seasonally to find food. Although the early Basketmakers

Bear Trail, Canyon del Muerto. Courtesy, National Park Service.

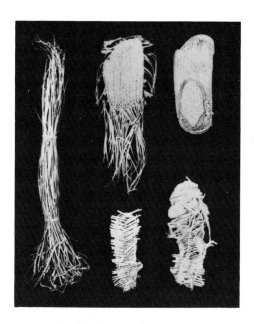

Sandals from Antelope House. Courtesy, National Park Service.

relied on corn and, to a lesser degree, squash as their primary foods, they still hunted antelope, deer, and rabbits, and gathered wild plant resources such as amaranth, sunflowers, and tansy mustard to supplement their diet.

The early Basketmakers also kept domesticated dogs and turkeys. Turkeys were kept both for food and for feathers, which were used for clothing and personal adornment as well as in ceremonial bundles. While dogs may have been eaten, they were primarily used as camp scavengers and for hunting game such as antelope.

The best-known early Basketmaker sites within the monument are Mummy Cave, Big Cave, and Battle Cove. Earl Morris's excavations at these sites yielded a number of Basketmaker storage bins, graves, and artifacts. Four early Basketmaker pithouses were excavated by Morris at Mummy Cave. One interesting discovery about the early Basketmaker people was that they often buried their dead within these caves, using old storage bins, or cysts, for tombs. The bodies were buried with their knees drawn tightly up to their chests, and they were wrapped in blankets or skins. In the graves were placed objects from everyday life, pottery vessels, baskets, and sandals. The dead were sometimes adorned with feathers and shell jewelry. Although many of these burials were disturbed by later inhabitants of the caves, a number of burials excavated at Battle Cove show evidence of violent death. This has led to speculation that strife existed between Basketmaker families.

While the early Basketmakers lived in the larger caves and on the plateau, they also used smaller caves and rock shelters to store grain in circular or rectangular bins made with upright sandstone slabs. The people filled these bins with corn, then sealed them with mud plaster to prevent insects and rodents from entering. Storage bins are found throughout the canyons, and many of them can be dated to this earliest Basketmaker period by tree-ring dates obtained from wood used in the construction of the bins.

The Basketmakers were good craftsmen and farmers. They wove fur blankets to keep warm and made fine baskets and sandals from plant fibers and twigs. Several important innovations, including pottery and the bow and arrow, as well as the cultivation of two new crops, cotton and beans, mark the beginning of the late Basketmaker period at around A.D. 500. The prehistoric population of Canyon de Chelly increased during the late Basketmaker period, thanks to the more reliable food supply provided by the increased number of agricultural crops and the improved hunting capabilities derived from the bow and arrow.

Pottery production most likely spread to the Four Corners region from Mesoamerica, reaching the Anasazi by way of their neighbors to the south, the Mogollon. Cultivation of beans may be related to the beginning of pottery production, because beans are cooked in vessels rather than parched and ground into flour like corn. The earliest Anasazi ceramics were plain graywares, but later pots were burnished with red ocre or designs were added with black paint.

The later Basketmakers continued to live in pithouses on the plateau and in large caves in the canyons, including Mummy Cave, Big Cave, Antelope House, Tse Ta'a, and Sonic Boom. Pithouses in these caves were generally circular, and were dug one or two feet into soil or rock. This provided insulation, serving to keep the houses cool in summer and warm in winter. The walls of the pithouses were cribbed with logs and tightly sealed with clay, with only a small central roof hatch as an entrance. A central firepit served for cooking and warmth, and low clay

Archaeologist collecting tree-ring specimens around Basketmaker II storage bins. Photo by Patricia Fall. Courtesy, National Park Service.

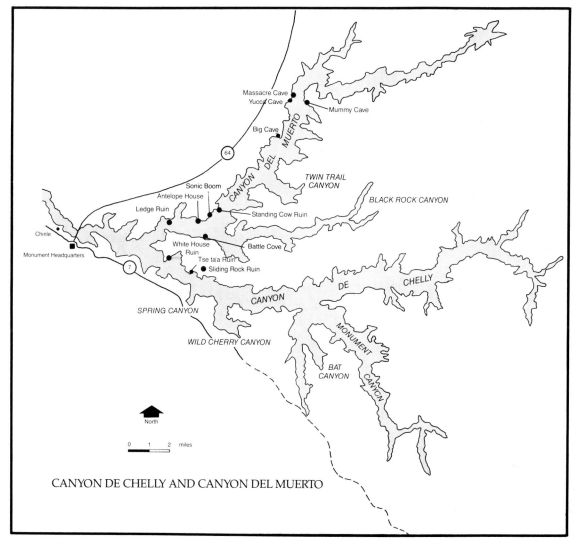

CANYON DE CHELLY AND CANYON DEL MUERTO

Map by Dany Walthall

wing walls partitioned activity areas within the structure. The size and configuration of these pithouses suggest that each dwelling was used by a single nuclear family. In addition, several of the larger late Basketmaker pithouses may have functioned as ceremonial centers or gathering places and may represent prototypes of later Pueblo kivas.

Late Basketmaker pithouses on the plateau were also circular and semisubterranean. Communities associated with them generally had one house, but sometimes had as many as four. Again, it seems a reasonable assumption that a nuclear family lived in a single house while extended family groups lived in several.

Although the Basketmaker people lived in small family groups, they may have had a larger sense of community, interacting and coming together with other Basketmaker families in Canyon de Chelly.

The Pueblo Period

Around A.D. 700 or 800, the people on the Colorado Plateau began to live in multiroom masonry pueblos. Unlike the pithouses of the Basketmakers, these homes were above-ground structures made of stone masonry or jacal (wattle-and-daub) construction. This latter technique involves placing upright stakes in the ground, weaving smaller sticks horizontally between them, and sealing this wall frame with mud plaster. The shape of the rooms also changed from circular to square or rectangular. These architectural innovations accommodated an expanding population as larger groups of people began to live together.

However, early Pueblo people of Canyon de Chelly continued to live in separate single-room domiciles: pithouses or structures made with large upright sandstone slabs as wall bases supporting wattle-and-daub upper walls. Their houses were still circular or rectangular with rounded corners. The early Pueblo people lived in communities of about the same size as those of their Basketmaker ancestors. It was not until about A.D. 850 that the Anasazi of Canyon de Chelly began to live together in larger population groups. Their villages were comprised of masonry and wattle-and-daub living rooms, but retained a pithouse, usually situated at the front of the pueblo, as a ceremonial room or kiva.

Although the early Pueblo period at Canyon de Chelly is not well understood, the results of extensive surveys of the Monument show that between A.D. 850 and 1050 the population was similar to that of the Basketmaker period; however, the people began to congregate in the canyons, living in the larger caves, including Antelope House, Tse Ta'a, Sonic Boom, Big Cave, Mummy Cave, and Yucca Cave. This reorganization of the population suggests that people were living in extended family groups, rather than as single families. This change in social organization may have been precipitated by a period of drier climate that drew people together and forced them to rely more heavily on agriculture and to depend on water resources in the canyons.

An interesting characteristic appears among the Pueblo people during the eighth century: the backs of their heads became flattened. Archaeologists originally believed that this phenomenon provided evidence for the arrival of a different group of people on the Colorado Plateau. They later realized that the flattened skulls were formed as a result of the custom of strapping the infants onto cradle boards.

The Anasazi of the early Pueblo period made white pottery by applying a white clay slip over their former grayware. They decorated these pots with black paint to produce the high quality Black-on-white style that is commonly associated with prehistoric Pueblo ceramics. Their designs were generally geometric, typical of the Kayenta tradition. During the ninth century the people of Canyon de Chelly began making corrugated pottery, first by leaving the coils around the neck of a pot unsmoothed, and later by not smoothing the entire outside of the vessel. The corrugations were made by pinching the unsmoothed clay coils together, sometimes making elaborate designs. The corrugations reflected a stylistic preference and also served to increase the surface area of the pot, allowing the contents to heat more rapidly over a fire.

On the basis of the number and size of archaeological sites, we estimate that the population of Canyon de Chelly had increased about sixfold by the period from A.D. 1050 to 1150, as compared to the preceding period from A.D. 850 to 1050. The Anasazi expanded their villages at Antelope House, Tse Ta'a, Sonic Boom, Big Cave, and Mummy Cave and began construction at White House, Battle Cove, and Ledge Ruin. They began building masonry pueblos on the Defiance Plateau. Their single-story stone masonry pueblos included living quarters, storage and work rooms, kivas, and open-air public plazas.

The Anasazi were now farming the canyons intensively, perhaps also dry farming the plateaus, and collecting wild foods from both environments. Their population increase may have resulted from their vigorous

Kana-a Black-on-white jar from Antelope House. Courtesy, National Park Service.

Corrugated utility vessel from Antelope House containing rock salt. Courtesy, National Park Service.

new agricultural economy, which culminated between A.D. 1050 and 1150. However, these were also years of more rainfall, a fact indicated by tree-ring studies as well as by analyses of fossil pollen and plant fragments excavated at Antelope House. Improved environmental conditions coupled with an exponential growth rate produced a veritable population explosion at Canyon de Chelly.

In addition to the often cited corn, beans, and squash, the prehistoric Pueblo people also consumed cactus fruits, beeweed, and piñon nuts. Beans were only a very minor component of their diet. Cactus and piñon pines may have been more productive during periods of increased rainfall. Cotton was commonly grown for fibers, and the Anasazi were adept at weaving cotton clothing and blankets.

Hunting continued to be an important part of the Anasazi's life. Wild game—rabbits, mule deer, antelope, and bighorn sheep—was about twice as important a meat source as the domestic turkey until after A.D. 1150.

The Anasazi of Canyon de Chelly traded with their neighbors from Chaco Canyon, Mesa Verde, and the Kayenta region. Pottery made by people living in the upper San Juan River and Chaco Canyon region was imported to Canyon de Chelly between A.D. 1050 and 1150. Because these ceramics were plain, unpainted wares, it has been suggested that the contents of the pots, rather than the pots themselves, were the focus of economic interest.

After A.D. 1150, the Canyon de Chelly Anasazi began congregating in large cliff dwellings in the canyons and no longer used the plateau as they had before. Decreased precipitation may have forced the people to rely more heavily on farming the canyon floor where, through irrigation, they could exercise greater control over a limited water supply. Irrigation may have required more centralized settlement and better coordination of labor as well as proximity to cultivated fields. These factors might in turn have contributed to the move to large cliff dwellings.

The number of villages of the Pueblo III period decreased, although some, including Antelope House, Mummy Cave, Sliding Rock, and White House, may have increased in size. These cliff villages characterize the Pueblo III period, with their large, well-built, multistoried houses. The walls were more massive than in previous times and were often constructed with a rubble core between two rows of stone masonry. Walls were sometimes plastered and painted, particularly in the kivas, which were central to ceremonial life.

The kivas were circular and subterranean, with a bench encircling the floor. A central fireplace was situated below the entrance hatch through which smoke was drawn by air flowing in from a floor-level vent. Most kivas had holes in the floor to anchor an upright loom. The weaving is thought to have been done by Anasazi men, for such has been the custom among the modern Hopi.

The influx of people to the larger Pueblo III villages of Canyon de Chelly may have been due, in part, to immigration from Mesa Verde and Chaco Canyon. The lower apartments at White House are built with the core and veneer masonry style typical of Chaco Canyon. The architecture of Tse Ta'a and Wild Cherry ruins also is Chacoan as are the ceramics found at these sites. At Mummy Cave, the central roomblock with its massive tower is reminiscent of the architecture of the Mesa Verde Anasazi. Some walls at Tse Ta'a were also built in the Mesa Verde style. However, the late Pueblo expansion at Antelope House was clearly not built by immigrants to the canyons. It has the same style of

Mesa Verde Black-on-white bowl from Antelope House. Courtesy, National Park Service.

*A kiva in Canyon del Muerto. Courtesy,
University of Colorado Museum.*

masonry construction that was common throughout the Pueblo period
at Canyon de Chelly.

About A.D. 1140 the people of Antelope House began major construction at the southern and northern ends of the pueblo. Don Morris, the National Park Service archaeologist in charge of excavations at Antelope House, suggested that the two roomblocks were made by two distinct social groups. His theory stems from the fact that the roomblocks are separated by a circular central plaza, and there are distinct differences in room construction, kiva wall art, basketry (coil size and stitch length), and ceramics (angle of indentions or corrugations). The people living at Mummy Cave and Sliding Rock also constructed two habitation areas separated by an open plaza or nonliving rooms, and White House is similarly separated into upper and lower living areas. Construction of the lower rooms at White House began about A.D. 1050, with the upper apartments being added around A.D. 1150.

Abandonment

The Anasazi lived in Canyon de Chelly for almost one thousand years. Their population increased only slightly between the early Basketmaker and early Pueblo periods, and then took a dramatic upswing in the century from A.D. 1050 to 1150. After 1150 the population declined, in spite of an influx of immigrants, and by the end of the thirteenth century the canyons were abandoned. What caused the Anasazi to leave the place that was their home for so long? A few clues point toward explanations for their disappearance.

Local drought caused the Anasazi to abandon their pueblos on the Defiance Plateau about 1150. At this time, some residents may have left the region in search of better farming land, but many settled in the canyon bottoms near water. They survived this dry spell from 1140 to 1180 by relying more heavily upon irrigation agriculture. The period from 1250 to 1276 again saw abundant rainfall; yet Antelope House was abandoned by A.D. 1270. Since the Anasazi had survived an earlier drought, the "Great Drought" of 1276 to 1299 would seem an inadequate explanation for their desertion of the canyons.

As larger groups of people lived together, they naturally had a heavy impact on natural resources, especially timber and firewood. The removal of trees and streamside vegetation would have promoted erosion and flooding in the canyons. Antelope House, which sits on the canyon floor, would certainly have been affected by stream erosion and flooding. Pueblos situated above the canyon floor, like Mummy Cave, were not directly affected by erosion, but associated fields would have been damaged. Mummy Cave was the last village occupied in Canyon de Chelly, but it too was deserted shortly after A.D. 1284. Thus two episodes of drought in the late twelfth and thirteenth centuries, separated by a period of erosion and flooding, combined with depletion of resources to force out the Anasazi.

Abandonment theories for the Four Corners region in the late thirteenth century have included disease, malnutrition, and warfare. The scenario for the disappearance of the Anasazi from Canyon de Chelly involves regional as well as local environmental conditions.

New towns became established in the Hopi and Zuni areas, and also along the Little Colorado drainage and the upper Rio Grande. The Anasazi had moved south joining other immigrants and creating Pueblo communities that have survived to modern times.

Mummy Cave tower. Photo by Patricia Fall.

The Canyons Today

The canyons have not been silent since the Anasazi left. Navajo people moved to Canyon de Chelly about 1750; their descendants continue to farm the canyons today. The Navajo came to the Four Corners region from the northern Great Plains and adopted a semisedentary life based upon an agricultural economy. They learned to grow corn, beans, squash, and melons from their Pueblo neighbors, with whom they sometimes intermarried. After the Spanish arrived in the Southwest, the Navajo became a pastoral society.

The Navajo today live on the plateau in small settlements or in the larger towns of Chinle and Tsaile, where they are closer to schools, shopping, and medical facilities. But they continue to tend their herds on the plateau and in the canyons, and to farm the canyon bottoms as the Anasazi did before them.

Pat Fall is currently a doctoral candidate in the Department of Geosciences, University of Arizona. She conducted archaeological research in Canyon de Chelly National Monument between 1977 and 1978.

The Narbona Panel, Canyon del Muerto. Photo by David Noble, 1985.

A MILITARY HISTORY
of Canyon de Chelly

By David M. Brugge

I T HAS BEEN close to half a millennium since Europeans first arrived in the Americas from across the eastern sea. Within three decades they had conquered the powerful Aztecs or, as they were sometimes called, the Mexica, and in little more than a century they ruled all settled peoples northward to the arid highlands of New Mexico.

As the Afghans set the western limits of the British Empire in India, so the Navajos set the western borders of the Spanish domain in New Mexico. This role was not readily apparent in the seventeenth century, when Spanish power extended, somewhat tenuously, as far as the Hopi villages. The great upheaval of the Pueblo Revolt in 1680 and the Spanish reconquest in the 1690s drew lines that effectively separated Christian from non-Christian for more than a century and a half, lines that became blurred at times, but were never completely broken.

Thus, the eastern regions of Navajo country were exposed to the threat of a powerful foe. Their residents welcomed Pueblo fugitives and refugees from foreign rule, as well as renegade peons trading stolen livestock. None who might help the Navajos maintain their independence were turned away, it would seem.

In the interior of Navajoland lay mountains and canyons unknown to the Spanish aliens. The two largest of these canyons were to gain renown, even though this recognition did not come until long after the Spaniards had become old settlers along the Rio Grande.

By 1720 Spanish empire-building waned and the accompanying wars of conquest had ended. Then another form of expansionism developed on the frontier, that of simple population pressure. As the colonists multiplied and as Indian numbers declined, new settlements were founded where peaceful relations seemed to invite them. The spread of white pioneers into traditionally Navajo lands inevitably led to conflicts over fields and range lands, conflicts that intensified as the newcomers' numbers increased.

CAÑON OF CHELLY
eight miles above the mouth.

Canyon de Chelly. Wash drawing by R. H. Kern, 1849. Courtesy, Academy of Natural Sciences of Philadelphia.

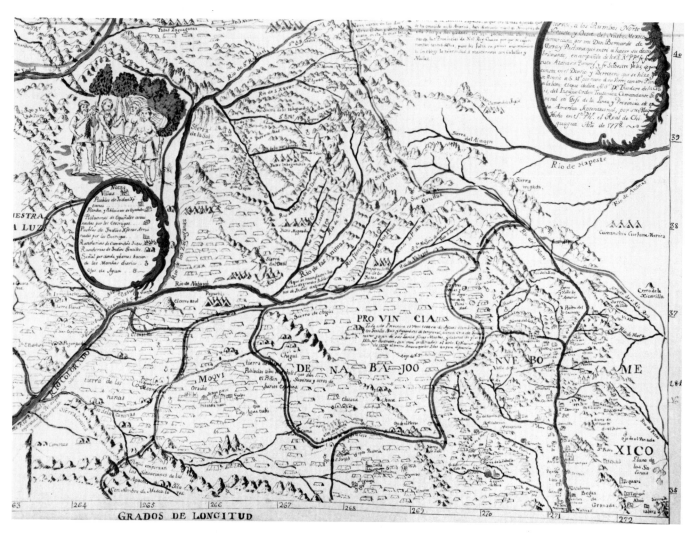

GRADOS DE LONGITUD

Map by Don Bernardo de Miera y Pacheco, 1778. Courtesy, New Mexico State Records Center and Archives.

The bilingually redundant name of Canyon de Chelly became significant to the whites only after the long period of peace between the Navajos and settlers came to an end in 1774. That year the Navajos drove back encroaching Spanish settlements and held their ground well during the ensuing campaign. Two years later Don Bernardo de Miera y Pacheco, a Spanish cartographer, took part in a long expedition that passed through Navajo country less than two days' travel south of the canyon. In 1777, he showed the place on a map for the first time. His knowledge of the name may have derived from this expedition or from the earlier war. The map shows miniature hogans beside a stream that he labeled "Chegui," but he provided no more detailed information. It is not clear whether he was aware that the name he used was a hispanicized version of *tséghi'*, the Navajo word for "canyon," a word that was soon further altered by the Spanish to "Chelli" or "Chelly."

Subsequent writings by Spaniards listed Chelly as one of the major Navajo population centers, but few, if any, colonists had actually seen the canyons. While relations between the two peoples returned to an uneasy peace, most white New Mexicans still knew only the place name.

For a large number of Navajos, the canyon called Chelly was home. The dependable streams watered corn fields and peach orchards, and the broken cliffs and promontories helped provide security from attacks by Utes, Comanches, Apaches, Spaniards, and other enemies. Not only did the local Navajo farmers find refuge within the alcoves and upon the rocky heights in the labyrinthine canyon system, but friends and relatives from more than a hundred miles away would retreat to this citadel when enemies threatened. United to fight on terrain that only they knew well, the men could repel any force that neighboring tribes could mount, while women and children remained quietly out of sight, concealed in a multiplicity of nooks, shelters, and fortified strongholds. Few were the raiding parties that had the temerity even to enter the canyons and fewer still those that dared stay long enough to inflict any real damage.

Navajo hogan, Canyon de Chelly. Photo by Ben Wittick, 1882. School of American Research collections in the Museum of New Mexico (neg. no. 16286).

With the beginning of the nineteenth century, Spanish settlers were again moving westward, grazing herds, plowing fields, and building homes in Navajo country. In 1804 the eastern Navajos rallied the entire tribe to the defense of their lands. Twice large and well-organized Navajo forces attacked the new white settlement at Cebolleta, but the firearms of the villagers deprived the Indians of a decisive victory. Smaller parties of raiders struck outlying Spanish sheep camps. The attacks were so devastating and the New Mexicans' response so unsuccessful that the commanding general of the Interior Provinces ordered a force of soldiers and Opata Indians from Sonora to their aid.

Antonio Narbona, the commander of the reinforcements, marched his men to Zuni, where he was joined by a detachment of New Mexicans and Zunis who assisted and guided him in Navajo country. On an excursion in November and December, they managed to overwhelm a small Navajo camp, surprised in a snowstorm. In January, however, the Sonorans and their local auxiliaries reached the canyons of Chelly, descended a steep trail, and moved down canyon until they located some Navajos on a "fortified point." Here, at what may have been present-day Massacre Cave in the canyon now called del Muerto, his men killed 115 Indians and took 33 captives, one of whom was Segundo, a headman from the eastern bands. Navajo resistance was spirited. The invaders escaped at the cost of almost 10,000 rounds of ammunition, 85 horses worn out and killed, and 65 casualties, including one death. Narbona's New Mexican auxiliaries returned to their homes with a new respect for the Navajos' abilities as warriors.

The Spanish continued to occupy Cebolleta, but their settlements spread no further into Navajo territory. In 1816 the eastern Navajos again sought refuge at Chelly, this time to escape Comanche raiders who were crossing Spanish territory to strike Navajo homes near Cebolleta. Suspicions of the settlers' complicity heightened Navajo fears. The governor of New Mexico denied any culpability, hoping to avoid another war, but the growing distrust on both sides could not be overcome so easily. The canyons' reputation as a stronghold made them a magnet for Spanish troops invading Navajo country. Few dared penetrate the inner canyon recesses; Narbona's experience gave ample reason for caution. The threat of Spanish attacks stimulated the Chelly Navajos to develop better defensive tactics than those traditionally employed against hit-and-run raiding parties. One tactic was to shift from large fortified home sites to smaller hidden or camouflaged homes with escape routes readily accessible. Many of these were built on ledges along the canyon rims. Another was a tendency for the people of the area to move closer to the canyons for security.

In 1823, José Antonio Vizcarra's troops skirmished with Navajos near the mouth of the canyon but elected to pursue Indians fleeing westward rather than brave the dangers of the canyon's depths. Even well-disciplined troops, when boxed in by close-set, vertical cliffs and harassed by warriors perched on the rocky crags, suffered disadvantages not experienced in open country.

Vizcarra probably made a wise decision, for he returned to Santa Fe with thirty-six captives and considerable booty in the form of livestock. After this campaign the Spanish initiated a trade in Navajo captives that would frustrate efforts at making a lasting peace for several decades.

Through newly opened trade with the United States over the Santa Fe Trail, the New Mexicans obtained weapons that provided them with such superiority of arms that war with the Navajo tribe was not feared as formerly. Subsequent campaigns seem, however, to have followed Vizcarra's lead and merely probed the environs of the canyons. Despite the whites' growing firepower, skilled archers posed a real threat where they could fight from cover at close quarters. One expedition in 1839 may have briefly entered the lower end of the canyons but quickly emerged to lay siege unsuccessfully to a nearby mesa where some Navajos had taken refuge. More devastating than the campaigns were the continuing raids by New Mexicans and Utes to capture Navajos to sell as servants in the villages along the Rio Grande.

Curiously the Navajos sometimes guided whites into their canyon in times of peace. Perhaps they reasoned that the impressive defensive advantages of the place would intimidate the enemy. In 1849, three years after the occupation of New Mexico by the United States, while Colonel John M. Washington negotiated a treaty at the mouth of the canyon with the headmen Mariano Martinez and Chapitone, some of his soldiers made a reconnaissance of the lower part of the main canyon, penetrating about nine and a half miles to the mouth of present-day Wild Cherry Canyon. At this time, a group of local Navajos displayed their nimble ability to climb on the steep-walled sides of the defile, duly impressing the Americans. It is probable that their intent was to show the intruders that the Navajos could easily dominate the canyons in the face of any attack.

In 1851, while leading the expedition that founded Fort Defiance, Colonel Edwin V. Sumner experienced the claustrophobia that frequently afflicted outsiders in Canyon de Chelly. After dragging cannon several miles up the sandy bottom, it was found that the balls could not reach the Navajo warriors harassing the column from the rims. One soldier later asserted that, while ineffective, the cannon fire had terrified many Navajos. Sumner's prompt withdrawal under cover of darkness suggests that it had been the American troops rather than the Navajos who were the more frightened.

The first recorded passage of whites entirely through one of the canyons since Narbona's time was made by Henry L. Dodge in 1853, shortly after he had assumed his duties as Navajo agent. Dodge, who had accompanied the 1849 expedition, observed a pastoral way of life, one more characteristic of the canyon than the hostile encounters usually recorded by military men. A local headman named Fairweather treated Dodge's party to green corn, melons, milk, and cheese. Amargoso, a war chief, also met them and invited a member of the group, a Reverend Shaw, to return when the peaches were ripe. Dodge's efforts produced a brief period of peace, an idyllic interlude that was but a calm before the storm of the final Navajo wars.

A lack of patience and restraint on the part of several American officials helped to precipitate the fighting, but at the root of the matter lay the grief of Navajos whose families had been broken by the loss of women and children to the slave raiders. In addition, peace meant a lack of captives to meet the demand for servants in the villages along the Rio Grande. There were those eager for war on both sides, and it took little to set it off. As was often the case in Indian wars, the earliest hostilities were intertribal. Utes, some-

Colonel E. V. Sumner. Courtesy Museum of New Mexico (neg. no. 11010).

times allied with Pueblo Indians and New Mexicans, began to raid the Navajos. One early attack, in January of 1858, struck at Canyon de Chelly where a local headman, Pelon, was killed. This may have been the raid depicted in the Ute Raid pictograph in present-day Canyon del Muerto.

By fall the U.S. Army was drawn into the fray as a result of the killing of an officer's black slave at Fort Defiance. One column of troops, led by Colonel Dixon S. Miles, made a foray down the length of Canyon de Chelly from the head of Monument Canyon. His daring was exceeded only by his haste to "get rid of this remarkable hole in the earth."

During the short peace of 1859, the Navajos reluctantly allowed a scouting expedition to explore the canyon from its head to its mouth. The report of the leader of this reconnaissance, Captain J. G. Walker, observed that the area's limited pasturage would prevent the Navajos from hiding herds in the canyon for any extended period of time. Like many before him, however, he failed to locate the Navajo's places of retreat on the more inaccessible heights.

Colonel Edward R. S. Canby, commanding the Navajo campaign of 1860, sent troops along both rims of the canyons but declined to enter. Captain Walker's report of the previous year would have offered a rationale for avoiding what gave all signs of being a most uncomfortable place to be in time of war with the tribe.

When Colonel Christopher (Kit) Carson embarked on what was to be the final campaign against the Navajos in 1863, he led his troops entirely around the canyons without coming close enough to see them, although Navajo scouts from the canyons doubtless saw him. The following January he sent two detachments into the canyons. One marched down the full length of del Muerto, the other up de Chelly. By this time the Navajos were badly worn

The Ute Raid panel, rendered in paint and charcoal, Canyon del Muerto. By permission from Canyon de Chelly: Its People and Rock Art, Campbell Grant, Tucson: University of Arizona Press, © 1978.

Left: Colonel Christopher "Kit" Carson, 1864. Courtesy, Museum of New Mexico (neg. no. 58388).

Right: General E. R. S. Canby. Courtesy, Museum of New Mexico (neg. no. 54169).

Below: Barboncito, a Navajo headman from the de Chelly area. Courtesy, Smithsonian Institution.

down by the repeated wars and raids; soldiers had destroyed their crops and run their herds off. Unceasing flight from enemies and camping without fire for fear of detection, left little time for productive work. Their ineffectual resistance to the troops in Canyon del Muerto consisted of a few shots, hurled rocks and insults, and flight to inaccessible heights. The soldiers killed two warriors and one brave woman whom they reported had "obstinately persisted in hurling rocks and pieces of wood at the Soldiers." The de Chelly column took many captives who were afflicted by malnutrition and wore only rags in spite of the freezing weather. This ease with which troops could enter the canyons seemed to be an important indication of the willingness of the desperate Navajos to submit. They were driven into exile and captivity at Fort Sumner (Bosque Redondo) on the Pecos River far to the east of their own country.

Within a few months more Navajos were marched to Fort Sumner than had been thought to exist. General James H. Carleton, military commander of New Mexico, was told that only the poor Navajos had surrendered. He hoped that when the rich Navajos appeared they would bring along their stock to feed themselves, for he had not the resources to care for all the prisoners. When the big Navajo stockmen came in, it was learned that the wars had stripped even them of their herds; Fort Sumner became a place of near starvation for all.

The canyons no longer could promise safety from enemies. Even those who escaped from the reservation spent little time there, for their homes and orchards had been destroyed. The hope that some caches of corn might have survived and that prayers at shrines might help alleviate their suffering drew a few back at this time.

In the spring of 1868, the Navajos successfully negotiated a treaty that released them from captivity and provided a new reservation in their old country. The chief negotiator on the Navajo side was Barboncito, a headman from the de Chelly area. Both he and another local headman, Hombro or Biwos, were among those who signed the treaty.

After the people returned to their canyon country in peace, they rebuilt their homes, repaired irrigation ditches, replanted orchards, cultivated fields in the bottomlands, and reestablished their flocks of sheep.

In the east, another war had ended. The Civil War brought an end to legal slavery and, with it, an increased sensitivity to the trade in human beings in New Mexico. Not only was raiding gradually brought under control, but in time some of the captives were returned to their own people. Wars with other tribes also became a thing of the past.

The world was changing and new questions needed to be addressed: should children attend the white man's schools? How should the white traders be dealt with? In what ways could the rapidly growing population be accommodated? Peace was not entirely certain even a decade after the treaty had been signed. There had been rumors of an Indian victory over the whites far to the north at a place called the Little Bighorn. The ideology of the Pueblo Revolt still survived among these heirs to the thinking of the Pueblo refugees who had refused to give in. There were some who proposed a renewal of warfare, but cooler heads prevailed. According to one story, the leaders of the faction promoting war were executed as witches. Biwos, who had signed the treaty ten years before, was one who died in the witch purge.

As the peace became ever more secure, the old places of retreat in the canyon were no longer maintained. Trails to the tops of the buttes and promontories were neglected, and it was no longer necessary to watch for signs of the approach of enemies. Still, the days of war are not forgotten. Rock art on the canyon walls depicts both invaders and defenders, and stories tell of the places where women and children hid and watched the soldiers ride by.

Navajos in Canyon de Chelly. Photo by Simeon Schwenberger, ca. 1900. Courtesy, National Park Service, Hubbell Trading Post.

David Brugge, an anthropologist and authority on Athapascans in the Southwest, is staff curator for the Southwest Region of the National Park Service.

Navajo farm, Canyon del Muerto. Photo by David Noble, 1981.

CANYON DE CHELLY
A Navajo View

An Interview of Mrs. Mae Thompson

by Irene Silentman

Mae Thompson. Photo by Irene Silentman, 1986.

Introduction

With the Navajo culture changing as it is today, much of Navajo life still revolves around storytelling. In the Navajo world view everything that meets the eye reflects the presence of *diyin dine'é* (gods and supernatural spirits). The gods brought the Diné (the Navajo people) up to this world and formed Dinétah (Navajo land) for them. Many such stories are told in the wintertime by elders who sit around the fire with their children, grandchildren, and relatives. They explain how certain landscapes came to be as they are today. If there are other elders present, then they reminisce and compare and exchange stories. New versions are understood and fitted into the missing sections of their own stories, so the process is like putting together a very complex puzzle. Many elders say this is a way of cleansing and renewing your spirits.

To listen to these stories in the Navajo language is an experience of unmeasured beauty, and an English translation, even of high caliber, cannot do justice to the powerful narratives. Many times the English translations do not capture all the special nuances of meaning expressed in the native language. The following interview provides us with several of the many stories of significant events and incidents of Canyon de Chelly.

IS: Tell me about yourself.

MT: They call me Mae Thompson. I am from this place called Del Muerto; the canyon's Navajo name is Tséyi'. I do not know when I was born. An older brother of mine who died not too long ago used to tell me that we were born one day apart. He was my aunt's son. He used to tell me that we were close to a hundred years old, but my (social security) card says differently. It says I was born in 1908 in July. I do not know which is true. My mother gave me the Navajo name of K'ízízbaa'. This is the name I am known by in my community. My clan is Hanágháanii. I have two older brothers still living and five children, two daughters and three sons. There are also several grandchildren. My husband died several years ago. I live here at this house with my youngest son and his wife; my other children have their houses around close by.

IS: Do you live here all year round?

MT: No. We live here only part of the year. Our summers are spent in the canyon. We have houses in the canyon that is called Black Canyon. The place we live at is actually near the mouth of Canyon Del Muerto and Black Canyon at a place called Tséláán. Our winters are spent up here.

IS: *When do you move down into the canyon?*

MT: It depends. Presently, our move into the canyon is determined by the water flow in the canyon. We used to spend only the winter season up here and move down into the canyon by spring when we only had horses and donkeys as our means of transportation. Now, our move depends upon the water flow. You see they open up Tsaile Lake and Tsééhats'ózí Dam in the spring and the water continues to run until midsummer. This is the reason why we do not plant until midsummer, which is really late. When this happens, then we do not harvest as much corn anymore, and we do not move into our homes until midsummer when the roads are dry enough to travel on. We enter the canyon now through Chinle. It is not like the old days anymore when we could use horses and donkeys. Now, we have trucks so we have to drive around Chinle. That is the way we also haul out our harvest.

IS: *What do you plant in the canyon?*

MT: We plant corn, watermelons, pumpkins and squash, beans and hay. We also have an orchard of peaches, apples, apricots, and plums, in addition to several grape vines. When it rains then we have an abundant harvest, otherwise it is usually small.

IS: *How long have you and your family been living in the canyon?*

MT: Ever since I can remember. We did not always live at this place where my house is now (on top). We used to live closer to the edge of the canyon near that hill (in the southeasterly direction from her house). One can still see the remains of our homes there. I can recall when I was a child. We were living at the bottom of the slope of that hill, and it was around harvest time when I saw several packed donkeys come up the horse trail with that fall's harvest. They were so loaded down with sacks and sacks of broken pumpkins. People used to do this at that time. They would break up all the pumpkins, pack them in large sacks, then load them onto donkeys to bring them on out to the top. Doing this made it easier to bring out the harvest.

IS: *When did you move to this area here?*

MT: My mother and younger sister were still alive when we moved here. I had just begun having children at that time. That was many years ago.

IS: *Did your parents ever tell you any stories about the canyon, events that occurred in the canyon or stories of people who used to live there long ago?*

MT: Do you mean the burnt homes in the canyon?

IS: *Yes, that plus stories of how people used to live long ago.*

MT: Those homes in the canyon were not burned by the Diné. Those ruins are Anaasází (Anasazi) homes. It

Mummy Cave, Canyon del Muerto. Photo by David Noble.

is said that when the Anaasází lived there, a big tornado came and destroyed them. This tornado came into the canyon from Chinle. It was a big whirling wind with fire. It went up each canyon and burned all the people. One can see these burnt areas today. They are those black bands and streaks on the cliff walls. They became this way from the fire and smoke. Everything in the canyon was destroyed, even the animals and all the vegetation. It is said that this whole area and the canyon were very thick with all types of vegetation and trees. The vegetation was woven with the trees, which made it very dense. It was lush and wild and jungly.

IS: *Why were the people destroyed?*

MT: They began to do and learn things beyond the knowledge that was set for them. It's like what is happening today. People began doing many abstract things, drawing and painting. Things became so abstract and intangible. This is why they were destroyed. Some of their paintings and drawings are still on the cliff walls. They made drawings of the wind, air, and all kinds of animals like cows, deer, buffalo, elk, and birds. They obtained knowledge beyond what was set for them. These are the stories of my father and my grandfather. My grandfather's name was So'nii'biye' (Son of the Star).

When I was about five years old, I remember Bilagáanas (white men) came into the canyon and began excavating, going through the Anaasází ruins. They dug up all sorts of things like clothing and bones of people and animals. I used to see all the things these Bilagáanas would dig up. They would lay them down for inventory before they would haul them out. It's amazing how the Anaasází lived. Their clothing was made of buckskin sewn with sinew, and they wore a lot of turquoise, chunky necklaces. I also saw combs (bé'ézhóó'), grinding stones, turkey skeletons, and pottery of various sizes. I don't know where the Bilagáanas took all their findings, probably back to their homeland. Yes, the Anaasází were destroyed because of their knowledge. They were afraid and built homes in the cliffs and walls of the canyon, but the gods did the worst that could be done to anyone, they destroyed the Anaasází with fire.

IS: *You say you live at a place called Tséláán in the canyon. Are there any stories related to this area that your kinfolk have told you that you want to share with us?*

MT: Yes. After the destruction of the Anaasází, the Diné moved in. They were living there happily until the Bilagáanas came in. The Bilagáanas would station themselves along the rims of the ledges and shoot at the Navajos. Many Navajos were killed and their bodies would just lie there on the canyon floors. This is why they took refuge on Tséláán. My grandmother, Asdzáán Das, was one of the ones who took refuge up there. There was another woman called Asdzáán Tséláán and many men who took refuge there, too. When the People climbed to the top of Tséláán, they dug an underground pit for hiding. When you see the top of Tséláán, there is no place where you can dig because it is all a layer of rocks, except for this one place. At the top there is a gap. In this gap is a small hill, and this is where the People made shelter and hid from the Bilagáanas.

Shots were coming from the different bluffs and ridges, and the People did not know what to do. A man named Dibé Yázhí Bich'ahí (The One With A Lamb Hat, so named because he wore a hat made of the skin of a newborn lamb) had an idea to trick the Bilagáanas. He put his hat on a long stick and waved it around from different positions, and the Bilagáanas would shoot at the hat. He did this so the Bilagáanas would use up their bullets. When this trick did not work too well, then Dibé Yázhí Bich'ahí and another man named Ch'il Haazhiní (Black Weeds Extend Out) decided to use witchcraft on them. They said if they did not do something then all the People would be killed.

Tselaan (middle-right in photo), where Navajos took refuge. Photo by Irene Silentman, 1986.

Across the canyon were some box-elders. The Bilagáanas camped here. It seemed as if they were going to be there a long time because they built a stone structure under the box-elders. They were going to subdue the Navajos by starving them. So it was that the two men began to perform the Witchcraft Way ceremony at dusk. They continued the ceremony throughout the night. During the night, one of the Bilagáanas yelled out, then another one and another. Pretty soon all of them were making noises, yelling, whooping, and cursing. It turned out that the captain was killed (witched) first. The following morning at dawn a young Navajo was sent to see what was happening at the white men's camp. He saw the men packing their horses, mules, and donkeys. They were leaving, so he watched them until they left the canyon. The Navajo ran back to the others and told them the happy news.

IS: *Who were these Bilagáanas? Were they cavalrymen?*

MT: Yes, they were cavalrymen. They wanted to kill off all the Navajos so they could take this beautiful land for themselves. It is said that they wanted to live here. However, they did not kill us all. Many Navajos hid in the high cliffs.

IS: *How did the Navajos get to these high cliffs? It seems almost impossible to climb up the sheer walls.*

MT: They used ropes to get down to the small cliff alcoves. They would put a stake at the edge of the cliff

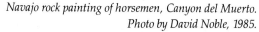

Navajo rock painting of horsemen, Canyon del Muerto. Photo by David Noble, 1985.

Navajo horsemen and deer, Canyon de Chelly. Photo by David Noble, 1985.

and use sash belts or yucca ropes to lower themselves to these alcoves. As they lowered themselves down to these alcoves, they made hand and toe holes (steps) with a rock called niɫ. This rock is a hard rock and was used a lot for hammering or digging. The hand and toe trails were made so the people could climb back up. Of course, they did not climb back up until all the Bilagáanas were gone.

IS: *What kind of food did the Navajos have with them in their places?*

MT: Not much. The one food that kept the Navajos from starving is called ts'áaɫbáí (shelled, steamed corn dried and ground to powder). They would have just a handful of this, compacted in lambskin pouches. The women carried this food with them all the time. During the times when the men went hunting and brought back meat, they would dry the meat and grind it to powder, too. This is what the men carried with them. They had very little food.

IS: *How did they get water up in those cliffs?*

MT: They used large gourds for water bottles. The tip at the tail end would be cut open, and the gourds would be scraped out that way. When the gourds were all cleaned, then they would cut pieces of buckskin to cover the openings. This is how they kept water. There is a story that after spending several months living in the cliffs the people ran out of water. There was no water to be found on top of Tséláán, so they had to go down into the canyon to get water. They used the ropes of sash belts and yucca to lower themselves down into the canyon at night. They filled all their water bottles with water at the water hole in the canyon and brought them back up. This is how the people overcame thirst.

IS: Did this event take place when the white men came and burned all the peach orchards and corn fields?

MT: Yes, that's right. This all took place around that same time. The white men burned all the orchards and fields. Many Navajos hid in the mountains—the Chuska Mountains. The white men rode up after them, but they were killed. The Navajos used arrows to kill them. They would climb on the trees and ambush the white men who rode past them. Many white men were killed with just bows and arrows.

IS: Is this the time the Diné were marched to Hwééldi (Fort Sumner)?

MT: Many events, including the stories I just told you, took place before Hwééldi. There is another story that occurred several years before. The Naakaii (Mexicans) used to come and steal women and children and/or capture Navajos for slavery. Those captured would be taken back to Mexico. One woman returned from there.

She was called Naakaii Asdzáán (Mexican Woman). Her mother was captured as a child, taken to Mexico, and was impregnated by a Mexican. Naakaii Asdzáán was born. She grew up to be a beautiful woman, light pinkish complexion and curly hair. She is now dead.

Soon after her mother died in Mexico, Naakaii Asdzáán became very homesick for her mother's homeland, so she escaped and started back. As a young woman, she was also impregnated by a Mexican boy, so there was a baby girl. She started off, carrying her child on her back, piggyback-style. After ten days of walking she saw that she was not gaining much ground and was becoming very weary and tired. She did not have any food with her except a small bag of ts'áálbáí. She drank this with water, you know, just enough to keep up her strength and keep her going. After ten days she could no longer carry her child anymore, so she threw the baby on the ground and stepped on her throat to choke her. The baby was crying at first, then she stopped. Naakaii Asdzáán took her foot off the baby's

Aerial view of Canyon del Muerto (left) and Canyon de Chelly. Photo by Paul Logsdon, 1985.

throat and started off on her journey again. When she was a few feet away she heard the baby let out a faint cry again. She returned to the baby, saw that it was still alive, and she just could not see her baby die there. She picked up the barely alive baby, fixed some ts'áálbái, and fed it to her. Then they began their journey again. That baby grew up to be a beautiful woman just like her mother was. She also is no longer alive, died an elderly woman. They used to live down there towards Chinle.

When the Diné were marched to Hwééldi, they were being blamed for raiding and stealing. On this long walk to Fort Sumner, some people walked, some rode on wagons, and some rode horses. It took many, many days before they arrived there. People spent several years there. Many wanted to return to their homeland, but the Bilagáanas would not let them. People begged and cried to be released to return home. The Bilagáanas are a mean people. Many Navajo women and young girls were impregnated by the white men, both Naakaii and Bilagáanas. When the People were finally released and started back, they had a lot of half-breeds with them.

IS: Did your parents go on this long walk to Fort Sumner?
MT: No, my father did not go there. These are stories that were told to him. My grandmother was one of the ones who went there. There are some trees in the canyon where we live that just fell last summer. It is said that the People were taken to Fort Sumner when those trees were very young. A couple of them were still green and standing when we left last summer. Maybe they will fall this summer.

IS: Are there any other stories that you would like to share with us? Perhaps you know of some stories of how the canyon (Canyon de Chelly) was formed.

MT: Yes. You did not ask me that, but I will tell you. My maternal grandfather said this story was told to him. A long time ago the canyon was not there. There are two versions of this. Some say the canyon was not there, others say it was already there. I will tell you what my grandfather told me. There was a big lake that formed by itself at Tsaile. In this lake lived a big monster called Deelgééd (a mythological monster similar to a rhinoceros*). I do not know what it was, but people have seen it. It would roar in a thunder-like manner saying "diil-l-l, diil-l-l." People say it did this when it was mad. One day it became very mad, probably at the People. The monster plowed open the lake, and the water rushed out and formed the canyon. This appears to be a very reasonable explanation for the formation of Canyon de Chelly, because one can see the water level that formed on the canyon walls. Today, it is still like that. You can see where the water level was. I think it's

true. When the monster plowed the lake open, the water made its way down toward that west mountain. Another lake formed there at the base of that mountain. The lake is called Tódiníhí (Water That Roars). The monster's roar was heard there again. It lived there for several years, then it moved on to Bilagáanatah (white man's land). I think this is true, too, that the water rushed down into Chinle and to the base of that mountain, because one can find those smooth water pebbles all along towards Chinle and all around there. There is a path that you can follow that leads to Tódiníhí Lake, and you find these pebbles all along there. It is said that the monster moved on to Na'ní'á Hótsaa (Navajo Bridge, Arizona). Now, people hear it roaring there, and we do not know if it will plow open that dam. However, no one has actually seen that monster in that area. I don't know what will happen.

Concluding Remarks

The home of Mrs. Mae Thompson and her family at Del Muerto, Arizona, is located across from Highway 64 above Antelope House Ruin and Standing Cow Ruin. Her children live nearby. She raises a few sheep and goats and has a small peach and apricot orchard. She also plants a small garden in the spring and grows several varieties of wild flowering plants. She planted the peach and apricot trees herself. The oldest tree is about three years old, and she says the fruit on this tree is very sweet and juicy. She informs me that many people buy or trade for the trees she plants. It makes her feel good that people come to her for her trees, because she feels she is contributing to their economy and welfare.

With her stories, Mrs. Thompson has provided us with another perspective—that of her people, the Diné. She has enlightened us with stories that have been passed down from generation to generation. Her stories illustrate to us that the world we live in was shaped by great supernatural forces, and that if we do not maintain harmony and balance with the supernaturals, the gods will become angry and alter the landscape again. In the stories the Navajos tell, there is always a moral to be learned.

Irene Silentman, assistant professor of languages at Northern Arizona University, is a member of the Navajo tribe. She has been working with the Navajo language and culture and bilingual education since the early 1970s.

Mae Thompson is an elder member of the Navajo tribe and a resident of Canyon del Muerto, Arizona.

---

*Interviewer's note.

Other titles on the National Parks of the Southwest:

Understanding the Anasazi of Mesa Verde and Hovenweep,
edited by David Grant Noble

Pecos Ruins, edited by David Grant Noble

Zuni and El Moro, edited by David Grant Noble

Salinas, edited by David Grant Noble

Wupatki and Walnut Canyon, edited by David Grant Noble

The Magic of Bandelier, by David E. Stuart

For further information on current prices and shipping charges, please
contact:

Ancient City Press
P.O. Box 5401
Santa Fe, New Mexico 87502
(505) 982-8195